TABLE OF CONTENTS

TIME TO UPDATE YOUR
LEADERSHIP PLAYBOOK

BRAIN SCIENCE FOR THE SOUL

AWARD-WINNING AUTHOR

ADRIANAVELA

IMPROVING THE HUMAN CONDITION

Foreword by Sandra Kay Helsel, Ph.D.

Edited and Published by SW Global Publishing (Pty) Ltd,
Cover design by SW Global Publishing (Pty) Ltd,
Image: The Elephant's Trunk Nebula by Beat Schuler,
Image: Blue and Green Peacock Feather Brain by Milad Fakurian

ISBN: 978-0-6452371-7-7

Legal & Disclaimer

The content and information in this book are consistent and truthful,
and it has been provided for informational, educational, and business
purposes only.

FOREWORD

It is an honor and a pleasure to introduce you, the reader, to Adriana Vela and her insightful book **Brain Science for the Soul**. I have known Adriana for more than two decades and continue to marvel at her ability to grasp the potential of fast-emerging technologies. She brings her unique interpretative capabilities to bear in this book--- with her analyses of neuroscience, leadership, and the human soul.

Early on, Adriana invited me to serve as the Director of Communication for the NanoBioNexus (NBN) organization she established in San Diego. I had been editor-in-chief of the Nanoelectronics.com news site as well as event organizer of that publisher's international events, and NBN was a perfect segue. I've spent my career in the communication of emerging technologies such as the early internet, virtual reality, carbon capture, 3D printing, robotics, and quantum computing.

I well remember Adriana's opening speech at the inaugural NanoBioNexus event and was struck by the obvious amount of research she had put into that presentation. I was deeply impressed at how she interpreted the present and future potential of nanobiotech to her audience. I had been evaluating and choosing speakers for international events for a decade by that time and instantly recognized the unique skills and content value she brought to her speech. As my tenure with NBN went on, I also came to appreciate Adriana's leadership effectiveness by observing her community- and business-building skills in action.

The same communication skills Adriana evidenced two decades ago are even greater now in this book, **Brain Science for the Soul**. She discusses the intricacies of the human brain, skillfully interweaving neuroscience with the art of leadership. The book is not merely a collection of theories but a practical guide that bridges the gap between brain science and the challenges faced by leaders today.

Today, I must also commend the in-depth research that Adriana has conducted for this book that is displayed in her citations and explanations from contemporary authorities such as Dweck, Covey, Rao, and Maxwell, etc. whom Adriana cites. Adriana goes deep in the book and explores the profound connection between our neurological processes and leadership effectiveness with precision and clarity. She discusses those contemporary researchers' insights, points out any misinterpretations of literature, and, importantly, also provides the necessary tools to implement. Her life experiences and her ability to communicate neuroscience research shine through in every chapter, offering a rare blend of scientific rigor and practical lived wisdom.

Each chapter of the book is a testament to the transformative power of understanding our brain's potential. The book covers a vast terrain of topics that are crucial for anyone looking to excel in leadership roles. The anecdotes, case studies, and exercises within these pages are not only intellectually stimulating but also deeply relatable, making the journey of self-improvement both engaging and achievable.

Adriana advises, "The world we live in is volatile, uncertain, complex, and ambiguous (VUCA), and it demands a new kind of leadership – one that is adaptive, resilient, and grounded in a deep understanding of human behavior." **Brain Science for the Soul** provides just that. It equips leaders with the tools and insights to navigate this landscape, harnessing the power of their brains to lead with confidence, empathy, and foresight.

The brain's non-physical counterpart is our soul, which leads us to ultimate happiness and peace. This book aims to empower you by presenting the magic of seeing the relationship between the two: brain and soul. More importantly, Adriana, via her narrative, shows us that our actions have a silent but direct impact on our soul, and taking care of it can awaken tremendous power in each of us. All we need to do is connect to it and **Brain Science for the Soul** shows us how to do that.

Importantly, in her discussion, Adriana shares her life's journey out of the physical and emotional *colonias* of Laredo, Texas. She refused to let the early circumstances of poverty determine her future. Adriana has shared her life's drive and wisdom in this book in her ever-continuing desire to be the best possible human and leader.

Sincerely,

Sandra Kay Helsel, PhD
SK Helsel & Associates

How I got here and why

In a family of thieves, the one that does not steal is made to feel shame.

It is, always has been, and always will be all about improving your odds.

Are you a gambler? If you're a high-achiever or go-getter, you are a gambler. If you're an investor, business owner, or executive, you're a gambler. If you're an entrepreneur or a visionary, you are a gambler. Even if you don't know you are one or go as far as denying it, you are still a gambler. You may ask, *'But what if I avoid risks and play it safe?'* You are still a gambler, but a pretty bad one at that! As you get to know me throughout this book, it will become clear why I start on that note.

As a young person trying to make it through life, I had to figure out how to achieve my first *pure intuition or gut feelings.* By 'pure' I mean untainted by unexamined biases I discuss later in this book. My earliest vivid recollection of gambling was at the ripe old age of seven, towards the end of first grade. While I did not understand much about life at that tender age, I was committed to one thing – I would do anything and everything I could to ensure I did not grow up like my mother. My mother did the best she could with what she had, but I wanted more for my life. Watching her struggle to feed us without support, always fighting to keep the wolf from the door, vulnerable and without resources. It sparked a deep fire inside me that I was determined to keep alight; a fire for having resiliency, love, joy, and abundance. One that would keep me from becoming a victim. I could not help her as a child but would later.

This drive is what brought me to this moment, to this point in my life, where I am excited to bring forth Brain Science for the Soul, a culmination of more than three decades of technology trends and application expertise, psychology and cognitive science research, and training and certification in behaviors, motivators, and emotional intelligence. Its purpose is two-fold:

1) To help you significantly improve your odds in the game of life, business, and leadership.

2) To reduce or eliminate the unnecessary suffering due to our evolving VUCA (Volatile, Uncertain, Complex, Ambiguous) world.

Even the strong need help.

It is foolish to think that you don't. Having conquered adversity, poverty, and abuse, I proudly consider myself a conqueror, but being strong and having the strength of wisdom is not the same thing. Learning from failures taught me to appreciate this distinction. Some people never become strong, and others never become wise. The result is either strong fools or unwise fools. You can prevent that from happening to you. The point was made crystal clear by the incomparable Les Brown, who says, "Seek help, not because you are weak, but because you want to remain strong."

Millions of people suffer and live unfulfilled lives because they miss this distinction. It does not matter whether you are intelligent or illiterate. It is not about knowledge but the courage to discover what's inside you. I find it mind-boggling how many people don't know themselves beyond their day-to-day preferences on food, apparel, entertainment, hobbies, and other areas of life. Most people run on autopilot, doing what societal norms tell them they should do. For example, have you ever considered exploring how you do the things you do and why you do the things you do? It is about truly knowing yourself in a Socratic way. Derived from the Greek philosopher Socrates, the Socratic method is a form of teaching that promotes critical thinking by focusing more on questions than answers. Hence, the quality of your life depends on the quality of the questions you ask yourself.

This book is not a panacea; however, it will assist with the transition from the knowledge economy to the new learning economy. It encourages giving yourself some grace if you experience a personal or professional failure and guidance on how to achieve that. It also helps you become comfortable with the fact that we are *perfectly imperfect*, and life always gives you a second chance – it's called TOMORROW.

I've always been insatiably curious and relentless in my pursuit to learn from the best. I was deliberate in my intentions and sought to surround myself with people who knew much more than I did. I instinctively understood why you never want to be the sharpest tool in the shed. It has served me well as it allows me to share this treasure trove of insights, education, and stories to simplify the integrative complexities between overlapping and often conflicting social perspectives, paradigms, human drivers, and how they shape us.

A universal question – How did we get here?

How did we even get ourselves here? I cover this in Chapter 6's section called How We Make Decisions. It's a question I have pondered for most of my life, but we are complex beings, and the answer is never stagnant. It changes because our perspectives change with time and new experiences. I asked myself this question at every critical junction while requiring myself to be grounded in dissecting the decision-making processes that led me to that junction. I instinctively studied the cause and effect of decisions because I thought avoiding mistakes, getting better at taking risks, and predicting outcomes were essential. For much of my formative years, it was a matter of survival. Sometimes it was life or death. This self-questioning served me well, and I came to believe that my pure instinct and burning desire would guide me to a different life than my mother's. It is about paying attention through observation and assessing by looking for signs of decision-making dissonance in my decisions and others' decisions and practicing beyond just getting it right.

Fundamentally, this describes The Dreyfus Model for adult skill acquisition commonly used to assess organizational competence. Yet, it is no different than learning to walk, ride a bike, drive a car, get your first job, or any new experience. Motivation, desire, and becoming comfortable with taking risks are vital to ascending through the five stages of acquiring new skills and improving your odds in life.

Stage 1 - Novice – A beginner with rudimentary information without reference to detecting errors or understanding if something goes wrong. From a competence perspective, this is similar to unconscious incompetence, where you don't know what you don't know. We've all been there, but each stage has essential distinctions.

- A confident novice embraces the beginner's mind and sees it as an opportunity for growth and learning new things. It is exciting. Innovators, leaders, creative problem-solvers, and lifelong learners are comfortable in this stage but intentionally focused on moving past this stage quickly.
- Unconfident novices embrace dysfunctional thinking patterns, fooling themselves by playing it safe and holding back. Whether it is ego or self-doubt, they fail to understand that playing

it safe has proven to be riskier, as evidenced by companies or people who lose touch with how the world has changed.

My gambling journey started at seven years old. I had no blueprint to work from, no guidance, role models, or mentor/coach for support. All I knew was what I later called my SWFF (Something Worth Fighting For). My burning desire would drive me to take more and more risks to figure it out every step of the way. Whenever I failed, I'd learn and try something else to reach the next stage and improve my odds. It is no different than progressing through the various stages of a video game.

Stage 2 – Advanced Beginner – Relevant connections and context grow through added knowledge and experience; however, there is no developed sense of practical priority between different aspects of work. You are still dependent on guidelines or others to lead and manage you.

- Confident advanced beginners know what they don't know but are aware of their progress and begin to make relevant connections in their environment. When they inevitably get tripped and fall, they see it happening, but they don't let their ego get in the way. They dust themselves off, dissect the cause, correct it, and try again.
- Unconfident people lack courage and accountability and succumb to the psychological pain of embarrassment, allowing the ego to

take over by blaming others for falling except themselves. They convince themselves they're not cut out for it and quit.

As a young child, I didn't care what others thought. I had not yet learned about the ego. All I knew was I'd figure out how to continue improving. My reward was learning to be a creative problem solver, which served me well in all future challenges.

Stage 3 – Competence – The amount of relevant information begins to feel overwhelming. Organizing it and developing a process to achieve your goals is necessary.

- Confident competence considers the time and effort it takes as an investment to gain efficiency and develop the processes to achieve effectiveness It is an intentional action for success and growth.
- Unconfident people see the task as a burden and become impatient and discouraged. They fail to see any return on their investment of time and effort, keeping them stuck at this stage.

At this stage, your mindset will either make or break you and keep you from achieving your goals. One of the tenets I live by came from my university's Handball Coach, who said, *Obstacles are what you see when you take your eyes off the ball.* It's true, on and off the court.

Stage 4 – Proficient – Intuitive diagnosis and application of insights to new problems take precedence over tediously following the rules. It is no longer a question of confidence. If you are here, you are confident in what you know. Instead, it is whether you are interested or committed to going further.

-   Being interested is when you start resting on your laurels. You stop innovating and default to what you already know. Phrases such as 'better the devil you know than the one you don't' or 'why fix it if it ain't broken' now factor in. Staying here is like stopping three feet from gold.
-   Being committed is when you know there is more because the world keeps changing. It is about growth and tending to your brain's planted garden to prevent weeds and pests from damaging it.

Stage 5 – Expert – Here you don't just know what you know, but you know *how* you know. You know exactly what to do and what it will take to do it. You trust your decision-making process and ability to develop creative solutions because you continue innovating. It is like being in a state of flow. You intrinsically understand that each situation is different and apply your expertise as a combination of knowledge and experience. In essence, you have possibly conquered yourself, despite yourself. The achievement and successes can become addictive as you repeat this process. The only caution here is not to allow your ego to hijack you into believing you are superior. Life is made of many areas beyond what you've conquered. Practice gratitude and share your wisdom with others who may benefit from it. It's about serving.

> *"We don't stop playing because we get old. We get old because we stop playing." – George Bernard Shaw*

In this book, you will also learn that many internal and external factors thwart your efforts, and sometimes, your brain works against you because of maladaptive conditioning. Maladaptive conditioning prevents you from adjusting in your best interest, such as avoidance, withdrawal, and passive aggression. You can't ignore it or sweep it under the rug. It will always be there until the experience is fully processed. The great news is that this can be undone when you learn more about how your brain works and how you can make it work for you. It gives me great joy to bring this book to you and inspire you to be in the driver's seat of your destiny. Consider this your GPS to success.

No fairy tale here.

My gambling ventures have always been driven by survival, self-preservation, and a penchant for escaping poverty and living the life I wanted and deserved. Even from age seven, I knew no magic fairy would help me meet my prince charming. Fairies and Prince Charming simply did not exist for me.

I was born in Laredo, Texas, a border town to Mexico. We had an outhouse for a bathroom, no hot water plumbing indoors, and we were raised on welfare and food stamps. My mother tried her best but was severely limited with only a seventh-grade education and an abusive husband who walked out on us and never provided child support. By the time I was fourteen years old, I was already working full-time during the summer and up to thirty hours per week after school during the school year. Out of necessity, I had to lie about my age, saying I was 16 because I had to help put food on the table.

Statistically, my destiny would've been to repeat the pattern of poverty given my environment, upbringing, scarce resources and opportunities, and negative role models – barefoot and pregnant, uneducated young women, continuing the trend of being a welfare mother. I don't think this was their true aspirations. So, how did I get here? Did my mom encourage me to fight for the life she never had?

Unfortunately, it was the opposite. My mom didn't know any better. The best advice she could offer was that I should learn how to cook and clean house so that I could get a 'good husband,' possibly reflecting on her own beliefs about failure. While her underlying intentions were good, they were misguided and doomed to perpetuate the cycle. My brain could see the cause-and-effect patterns. Many battles would ensue as I refused to go with the program; after all, what good daughter would not listen to her parent? Perhaps I was not grateful that she had brought me into the world: *bad daughter, bad daughter* is what I'd hear. I would forever feel like the black sheep of the family—the rebellious, defiant, and ungrateful one.

But this was not her fault. She was a product of her upbringing. My grandmother was unkind and a stern disciplinarian. I heard many stories from my mom and aunts about what it was like growing up with her and how she would yank big clumps of hair out of my aunt Elisa's head, her first child. She was physically and psychologically abusive. I never met my great-grandparents, but I remember my mother, the second-born after Elisa, saying my great-grandma was also mean to her when she was a child. Perhaps this is why mom was not horrified when my grandma said right to my face that I was ugly and nobody wanted me. Were my feelings hurt? Was I crushed? I can't say I was. It was a strange and twisted blessing in disguise, perhaps because nobody had convinced me that I was pretty or wanted me to begin with. Criticism and insults were all the attention I received, after all. My mother followed the same pattern as Grandma. It was the norm, but I did not want that to be my norm.

Visiting Grandma was never fun. My mom was often upset when we'd leave Grandma's because her attempts to try and get some financial support were always denied. Grandma was punishing and made her feel unworthy and alone as she pointed out her failures. After all, she couldn't keep a husband, so what good was she? is what

I often picked up on. Yet the one she 'couldn't keep' was the one that would beat her and force her to wash his shirts that had another woman's lipstick on the collar. He abandoned her and refused to support his son, my oldest brother. Her mother-in-law shamed and blamed my mom and turned a blind eye to the injustice, pain, and abuse her son caused, saying she must've deserved it. Starting to get the picture?

Was this just a result of lousy behavior patterns? A resignation that this was how it's always been, and that they don't know any different? Or was it that life for impoverished women then was so hard that it made them bitter and angry, and they felt the need to take it out on their children? Especially if they looked a lot like their father, as I did. Was it a sign of the times when women could not challenge their husbands because they would quickly be put back in their place with a beating? Growing up, I witnessed this type of treatment from some uncles toward their wives. I never saw any sign of my grandpa being mean to Grandma. He was a thinker, not a drinker, but my uncles were, and that's when they were at their worst.

Grandpa, on the other hand, was never mean to me. He was always trying to teach common sense. He was a modest and kind man who treated all his grandchildren the same. He'd hug us all, and we all got a nickel allowance.

He encouraged the concept of saving it for 'a rainy day' and not spending it right away on candy. I think I was the only one who saved my nickels, literally burying them in the backyard as one would a treasure. I was nine years old, and my goal was to save enough not to be or feel poor. It was part of my grand plan for a better life, and burying it reflected my need to hide it from others around me as I knew it would be taken. This was part of my mental grounding, like a map that would guide me back to it if I got lost along the way.

I would consistently observe my grandpa trying to adoringly flirt with grandma while she would blow him off or outright reject him. My grandfather was my only father figure. I always appreciated Grandpa and miss him terribly. Grandpa was mathematically brilliant even though he only had a second-grade education. He worked his way to become the senior accountant for a hardware business. This may not mean much to most educated people, but consider what this meant for a young, uneducated man. I met the CPA who handled that company's account when I was a young adult. He told me he knew my grandfather well and was the only person he respected and trusted with the books. Grandpa was also musically talented and taught himself to play five instruments, including the violin, and write music just by ear. Later, when I took an accounting class in college and had to purchase the HP35 financial calculator, I would race Grandpa on net present value or percent margin calculations I would do on the calculator while he did them in his head. He was quicker, so, no, I'm not exaggerating. He was brilliant, humble, and such a positive influence. I respected him immensely and am grateful I had him while I was growing up.

My dearest aunt, Elisa, the oldest, was never mean to me either. As the firstborn, I later learned that she had given birth to a child out of wedlock and that Grandma had forced her to give it up for adoption. The choice was to give it up, or she'd be disowned and tossed on the streets. My aunt dedicated her entire life to serving my grandparents until they died and all five of her brothers until they all married and moved out. While the grandparents were alive, she was expected to still serve her brothers when they visited.

My aunt Elisa is an unsung heroine. Not for her ability to serve but for her ability to live a cruel life of servitude and not become bitter. She was the only family member who believed in me and encouraged me to make a life away 'from all of this.' She'd continue with, 'You have what it takes.' On the other hand, my mother exhibited patterns of severe insecurity and victim behavior on top of the culturally driven brainwashing. She rejected the thought of me leaving, not knowing who would take care of her. She was paralyzed with fear, shame, and unworthiness. My aunt was my angel then and still is, even after she passed 25 years ago. She was a beautiful soul, and I still miss her to this day.

It is hard to describe how much of a positive influence she had on me. Her courage, love, and capacity to forgive despite her circumstances made her a superhero to me. While others would break, she was stronger because of it. They took everything from her except for her kind soul. To this date, I firmly believe that I would have been lost if I had not clung to the light from my Grandpa and Aunt Elisa. They gave me the strength and courage to fight for a better future.

What I know the most s what I experienced directly and observed diligently. Most adults don't realize just how much children pick up and capture about what is happening around them, even if they don't understand it. I saw how miserable my mom was, how hard she worked raising us, how defeated and unworthy she appeared, and how educationally limited she was. She would share stories of injustices she experienced, like getting fired from a job at a soda shop because she had to bring my eldest brother with her since she could not afford to have somebody watch him. She'd sit him in a corner and would not move a muscle. Her boss, a cranky bastard, given the story, said he didn't want her to bring him because he looked like a beggar, and it would deter the customers. The ultimatum was: *"Either come back without him or don't come back at all."* I never heard a story where she had not suffered an injustice. She was not an evil person. She was merely a wounded and damaged soul. As a child, I was powerless to help her. Seeing this, however, sparked my burning desire to be strong and capable. To do everything I could to ensure different outcomes. To fight back against injustices where she couldn't. To refuse to be a victim where she couldn't. To become educated and figure a way out of obstacles where she couldn't.

I have no idea whether the word 'bullying' existed when I was growing up, but I can tell you that it was par for the course. And because of all that I observed during those formative years, I was somehow compelled to take on schoolyard fights on behalf of scared kids bullied by more aggressive kids. I'd step in to protect the scared kid because I knew what it was like to feel defenseless, and I didn't want the aggressors to get away with it. At that moment, I had no idea if I would win the fight, but I knew I'd draw on my conviction not to be a victim. The strength of conviction can be mighty. I noted that and was victorious at least 90% of the time. It felt good to 'right the wrong' and teach bullies a needed lesson, even if I didn't know the kid I was defending. It also did not matter to me if the aggressor was a boy. I could not let that stop me because it was still wrong. I recall one fight where a boy wasted no time and punched me in the stomach so hard I folded over. I guess he thought he had 'put me in my place'— typical of bully behavior. What shocked him was how quickly I stood up and faced him again. My stomach was hurting, but I was not going to give him the satisfaction of showing it or throwing in the towel. He would not be victorious because I would not be a victim. I laugh when I think back to his 'oh shit' expression, followed by fear and confusion. I must've had a look about me that spelled, *You don't scare me*, because he and his cheering friends ran off. I laugh even more imagining myself as a female child version of Lucifer Morningstar, played by Tom Ellis in the wildly popular TV series *Lucifer,* when he was about to teach a horrible person a lesson.

No matter what I sought to learn, I was always focused on fine-tuning it until I had it wired. I vividly recall the first time we moved into the low-income housing projects. I was eleven years old and thought somehow we had made it big! Why? Because we had a flushing toilet inside the house, hot water plumbing, and an actual shower and bathtub! Jackpot! It was a vast improvement from the outhouse and bathing under a faucet in a galvanized tub where mom washed clothes with water heated on the stove. The walls were solid concrete blocks with no holes where snakes could slip in. I appreciated what, at the time, felt like luxury. As I think back to that moment, I was exhibiting gratitude for what I had at the time and celebrating the small progress.

Along the way, I also had to battle my mom to stay in school and graduate. I deflected any sabotaging when I tried to study late because she feared the electric bill would be too high. This, even when I was already working and contributing to the household. As a teenager, I'd have to leave the house and go to Denny's, a twenty-four-hour diner, and sit there doing my homework as other high schoolers would come in after a game or party. I was a bit self-conscious being there alone doing homework, but I decided that I would not let that stop me. I remember telling myself: *Don't focus on them; focus on what you need to do and get it done.*

My formative years laid the foundation for knowing what I didn't want for my life, even before identifying what I did want. I knew I didn't want to grow up and be like my mother. I didn't want her educational achievements, earning opportunities, relationships, assets, victimhood, and certainly not her damaged maternal methods.

I kept my eyes on the ball every single day, learning as much as possible to sustain myself and live my life on my terms. I'm living proof of Bill Gates' quote: 'If you are born poor, it is not your fault. If you die poor, it is.' Remember that 'poor' can mean your attitude, your alignment with your values, and the legacy you leave behind.

What will be your legacy? How do you wish to be remembered?

I've been using the metaphorical gambling term to shift the perspective towards taking smart chances. It is not easy dealing with uncertainty, but Newsflash: life IS uncertain. There weren't any guarantees handed out when you were born. There are no guarantees now, and you'll find none in the future. Fearing uncertainty is nothing more than a setup for emotional fragility, chronic stress, anxiety, and a disappointing and miserable life.

In the following chapters, I'll share stories beyond these formative years throughout the book to illustrate key points. For now, what's uber important is to believe in yourself enough to take the necessary chances to free yourself from unnecessary pain and suffering. To break the chains that hold you back and the unconscious sabotaging you've been unaware of. To live your life, drive your career or business on your terms, and never become the victim.

Hence, one of my favorite quotes:

"I am not a product of my circumstances; I am a product of my decisions." – Stephen R. Covey

I decided not to dwell on anger at the memory of the abuse I suffered as a child. Not because I think I'm a saint but because it is a colossal waste of time that yields nothing good in return. As a consummate problem solver, I had better things to work on. Besides, I had vowed never to play the victim. I moved on and was better for it. Or was I?

"Do not kid yourself. A conflict is never about the surface issue. It's about the ones unsaid, untreated, and unhealed wounds" - Unknown.

Here's the catch: while I moved on and did well for myself, I eventually learned the stealthy negative impact unresolved trauma has on you until it is resolved. It is like a slow-growing infection lurking and festering below the surface until another problematic situation or trauma ignites it. Investing in yourself to discover hidden gems by cleaning out your YOU closet pays dividends for this exact reason: to free yourself and design the life you want and deserve.

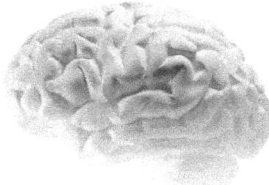

CHAPTER 1

YOU THINK YOU KNOW YOURSELF - THINK AGAIN!

What is Brain Science, and why is it important?

Our very humanity depends on brain science. Allow me to explain. From a strict definition perspective, *brain science (noun) is a branch of neuroscience concerned with the brain's functional processes.*[1] In my practice, the brain's function relates more to cognitive science and cognitive psychology, which pertains to the mind and its processes-in other words, how it works. Brain science is an exciting interdisciplinary field because it includes contributions from neuroscience, psychology, linguistics, philosophy, computer science, anthropology, and biology.

Now let's define the soul. Merriam-Webster defines the soul as the spiritual or immaterial part of human beings

---

[1]   https://www.thefreedictionary.com ›brain+science

or animals regarded as immortal.[2] A second definition for the soul is an emotional or intellectual energy or intensity, especially as revealed in a work of art or an artistic performance. For example, "Their interpretation lacked soul."

The word soul is used in many different ways. Large companies are often called soulless corporations when they're all process and no heart. When someone says that a person has a beautiful soul, they usually refer to a person with a kind, giving nature, someone confident, genuine, balanced, and understanding. People with beautiful souls make others feel safe and at peace.

The idea of an intersection between brain science and the soul has fascinated me because it has not been explored side-by-side. I closely observed others' words, behaviors, and actions to find meaning and later spent years on focused research and study in this area. It's the reason I established my mission to improve the human condition. With my background in technology and deep study of neuroscience and behaviors, I blend the two to create a holistic approach to getting the most out of life and achieving everything we are capable of. My background in computer science has taught me to look at systems, and I look at brain science and the soul as part of one system. I believe we can improve the human condition through

---

2   https://www.google.com/search?q=soul+meaning&rlz=1C1N-HXL_enUS682US682&oq=soul+&aqs=chrome.1.69i57j35i39j0i 433i457i512j69i59j0i402l2j0i433i512j69i60.9496j1j7&sourceid=-chrome&ie=UTF-8

scientific understanding of technology and systems, right down to the level of our souls. If we understand this and how our brains work, then in combination, we can create our own roadmaps to whatever we want to achieve, which is ultimately the soul's journey.

Linking brain science for the soul with technology systems and cognitive science allows us to achieve a soulful mind that brings us and others toward peace, safety, and harmony with ourselves and others. Suffering and unrest do not have to be in your future.

Socrates, the father of modern Western philosophy, said, "An unexamined life is not worth living." To live the best life, we need to understand ourselves better, not just from our cognitive functions but also our soul functions. When we can make this junction work together, we achieve grounded harmony and what we most desire.

My point is that most people think they know themselves, but they don't. I see this all the time when I work with clients. They experience many AHA moments when they finally understand the 'why' of their behaviors, thoughts, biases, and blind spots. How could they truly know themselves when there is ingrained avoidance of introspection or self-reflection because it is fraught with pain and maladaptive behavior patterns? This means your behavior prevents you from adjusting in your best interest. Earlier, I mentioned avoidance, withdrawal, and passive-aggressive behaviors, but others include self-harm, anger, and substance use to ease anxiety or stamp painful feelings.

Adaptive behavior is making the choice to solve a problem or minimize damage. In contrast, maladaptive behavior patterns lead to becoming comfortably numb to those patterns, even if they're harmful—for example, the tendency to outright deny that issues exist or refusing to see them. If you accept being diminished or settling for living your life like this, it says that you are not worthy, not realizing that these beliefs grow to become self-fulfilling prophecies. You give up your agency to do something about it because you're scared it will hurt, but there are ramifications for not dealing with what's beneath the surface of your consciousness- that which is damaging your soul. This is a bigger tragedy because the fact is that you are worthy. Stay with me and I'll show you.

So, have you met the real you?

If people can overcome their fears and be brave, not only will they be happier in their own skin, but they will have a positive impact on the world around them and everyone they meet. They become beacons of light atop dark cliffs, guiding others toward hope and peace. Overcoming, no matter how hard it may seem, is food for the soul, and the soul must be fed, or it will die of hunger.

We are responsible for doing this for ourselves because we live in a world of constant change and disruption. To keep up, to not only survive but thrive, we absolutely need to explore and understand how we work from our brain's perspective and create new patterns and mental models that help heal the soul and allow us to be happier.

Based on trends and observations over the last three decades, humanity is slowly eroding its soul. It's been trampled because of how we make decisions in a constantly volatile, uncertain, complex, and ambiguous world - a concept known as VUCA.

The Army War College first introduced the concept of VUCA to develop strategic leaders after the Cold War ended in 1897. The concept was later applied in the business world where it took root as emerging ideas in strategic leadership.[3]

The only way to avoid the consequences of VUCA is to sit firmly in the driver's seat of our destiny. To get there, you must know how to navigate uncharted terrain – your brain and entire self. More specifically, I'm referring to the discovered, grounded, and empowered YOU. It's about learning how to make unexpected disruptions work for you because this is how you will survive in our constantly evolving VUCA world.

---

[3]   https://usawc.libanswers.com/faq/84869

What if you're wrong about everything you've ever thought?

I know that sounds scary, but it's not as if I'm asking you to choose whether you want the red pill or the blue pill (The Matrix movie, anyone?) Don't worry, it's much less dramatic than that. The point is that before we learn anything new, we have to unlearn a lot of myths that we have all grown up with and adopted as our worldviews. For example, one of the biggest lies that science has taught us in the past is that we, as humans, have three brains.[4] Lisa Feldman Barret is a Professor of Psychology and a neuroscientist at Northeastern University, and her research has uncovered that our brains don't work the way we have been taught they work.

Today, we know that the human brain has an estimated 128 billion neurons, and from those neurons, multiple trillions of patterns that develop based on our experiences are created and managed.

Most people don't realize that most of what we learned in school about how the brain works and how it evolved is false. The fundamentals we were taught say that the brain has three dedicated areas that serve specific functions:

- the neocortex or rational brain
- the limbic system or emotional brain

---

4   Feldman Barret, Lisa. "Seven and a Half Lessons About the Brain." HarpersCollins Publishers, 2020.
     https://usawc.libanswers.com/faq/84869

- the survival system or lizard brain

From an evolutionary perspective, the story was that we evolved in three layers – one to survive, one to feel, and one to think, giving way to the triune brain concept. This notion was formalized in the mid-twentieth century by physician Paul MacLean. The theory was entirely based on visual inspection of various lizard and mammalian brains using a microscope and noting similarities and differences. No other evidence was provided to promote the triune brain concept. Sadly, you can still find these disproven terms embedded in some teachings today.

Dr. Lisa Feldman Barrett puts it like this, "The triune brain idea is one of the most successful and widespread errors in all of science."

Another fallacy is that the human brain has dedicated areas for very specific jobs, such as the ocular area of the brain, which is responsible for translating everything that comes through our eyes. Then there is another part of the brain that only deals with our emotions, and one for sensing and reacting to external stimuli like goosebumps or the hair on your arms standing up that signals the brain to prepare us for fight or flight. There are more but think of it this way – these sensory areas of your brain are like the instrumentation panel of a major airline cockpit which informs the pilot (brain) what is happening so that it can make the right decision to get to the intended destination and land the plane safely. Unlike the instrument panel, these brain areas are not dedicated because the brain figures out how to rewire the neural pathways to compensate when one path is unavailable. For example, if you lose your eyesight, the brain strengthens other areas – expanded hearing abilities and finger sensitivity to read braille. Our brains are truly amazing, but first we need to unlearn these fallacies and other common myths before upgrading and training our brain for peak performance.

How did the brain evolve?

Contrary to popular belief, the brain is not for thinking. It's for predicting. As humans, we are considered to be at the top of the food chain; therefore, our superpower is our ability to think. This is what school taught us, but this is not the case. Our brain did not evolve to think. Our brain is a command center- it evolved to be more and more complex because our physiology is more complex. Because our bodies have so much complexity, the brain needs to adapt to become more efficient and predict what will happen next and what the body will need. The ability to think was not its primary purpose. Dr. Feldman Barret's body budgeting concept explains the greater need to manage billions of neurons and hundreds of thousands of chemicals, such as water, salt, glucose, and much more, coursing through our body. The brain meters these: are you gaining or are you losing? It determines whether you have enough every second of every day.

The Cambrian period, which began 541 million years ago, is acknowledged as the most intense burst of evolution ever known, ushering in an incredible diversity of life.[5] The brains of creatures in this period were very simple. All they had to worry about was, *Is that blob in front of me going to eat me or not?* More complex brains appeared 500 million years after animals exhibited the ability to hunt one another. The animal's survival and evolution were based mainly on agility and efficiency. The animal would either move very fast and take the meal or move fast enough to escape becoming a meal. All creatures continued to evolve- birds, reptiles, fish- and all became smarter, using more faculties, but for the brain, it's all about body budgeting to make every bodily process more efficient so that the body has what it needs to survive. Your brain's most important job is not thinking- it's running your body's energy budget! Energy efficiency is, therefore, the absolute key to survival. Being efficient allows you to survive and thrive—the brain's number one job. If you are curious, the number two job of the brain is to procreate. Thinking comes in somewhere after that! Dr. Lisa Feldman Barrett describes it as, "*Every action you take, or don't take, is an economic choice. Resources are either withdrawals or deposits. Certain activities, like running or swimming, will use up (withdraw) resources, and others will replenish (deposit) them by eating and sleeping.*"

---

5   https://www.nationalgeographic.com/science/article/cambrian

From the moment you are born until you take your last breath, your brain is managing your bodily resources 24/7, 365 days a year. As a brain science consultant and coach, I help my clients understand more of what goes on in their brains to gain a deeper understanding of their brains' complexity and fantastic power as illustrated in the 24/7 Biological Symphony below. From there, we focus on managing across a spectrum because nothing is finite or black and white. They learn to navigate with precision and sit solidly behind the wheel towards achieving their goals.

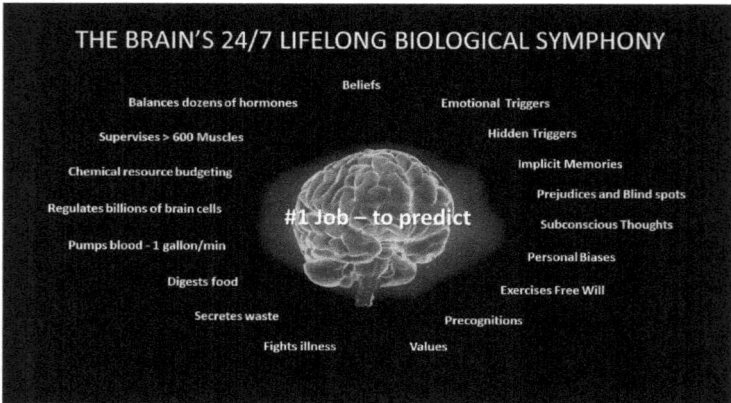

THE BRAIN'S 24/7 LIFELONG BIOLOGICAL SYMPHONY

Balances dozens of hormones
Supervises > 600 Muscles
Chemical resource budgeting
Regulates billions of brain cells
Pumps blood - 1 gallon/min
Digests food
Secretes waste
Fights illness

Beliefs

#1 Job – to predict

Emotional Triggers
Hidden Triggers
Implicit Memories
Prejudices and Blind spots
Subconscious Thoughts
Personal Biases
Exercises Free Will
Precognitions
Values

Unlearning myths about the human brain

Myth 1: Specific brain regions have dedicated functions. As mentioned earlier, it was believed that specific brain regions, such as the ocular area, exclusively took charge of the visual processing of information that comes through our eyes. That is not the case. The way neurons work is that whichever neuron is available is the one that will take in the information and process it, as proven through research and scans of visual experiments. The visual experiments include observing where activation occurs in other brain parts outside the ocular area when taking in the visual information. Metaphorically, it's like different taxi companies lined up at the airport, ready to 'deliver' passengers to their destination.

The brain does not react to internal stimuli. Your organs have sensors, and these sensors sound alarms. For example, a person with an ocular migraine may think the brain is responding to over-stimulus through the eyes; however, the eyes are merely sounding an alarm. And that alarm is the headache that says, *I need 'this.'* The brain does not react to *'this'*; it is already preparing for what the body is going to need. It will drive the action you need to take to quiet the alarm. This function can occur anywhere in the brain.

When you have a stomachache, the way patterns work is that the brain observes the context of what's going on- maybe the stomach's uneasy because you're in an area that's dangerous. If it's fear-driven or safety-driven, the brain takes all that input and matches that pattern to any other experiences you've had or witnessed. The brain remembers the pattern it had developed, and it will raise your heart rate, raise your cortisol, and put you back into that state of arousal to get yourself to safety to survive. The brain does not react to it; the brain makes you react based on the input and previously established patterns.

In a different context, the same pain in your stomach could sound the alarm if you were giving a speech in front of thousands of people. Fear, nervousness, and even love all create the pattern that we call butterflies in the stomach, patterns previously established throughout our early developmental stages. The brain gives the body what it needs for its context, either raising the cortisol to run fast for safety or smiling and blushing to create a love connection. Our brain assesses how to deal with the situation and provides the resources for reaction and action based on pattern recognition and predictability.

The brain's action is the firing of the neurons based on its predictions. All the brain is doing is predicting what might happen. It uses past experiences as a reference, patterns previously established. It's like a cue where the brain says, *I've been here before, and this is scary, so let me get out of here.* The neurons fire to achieve whatever action needs to be taken to reach safety. And this happens 24/7. Have you ever had a dream where you wake up and drenched in sweat, your heart racing? You weren't there, but your brain detected a pattern based on visions based on the memory of something you saw or were thinking about, even in a sleep state.

Countless experiments debunk the myth that this kind of reaction happens only in the fight or flight part of the brain, the cerebellum. The brain is not interpreting the sensors. It is responding to them. The brain looks at these sensors and says something is wrong. For example, you cut yourself or stub your toe, or you have a headache, and based on experiences, your brain is preparing to release chemicals in some area, trying to anticipate what the body is going to need. And if it needs to, it's going to signal and create actions in your body so that you can take the necessary steps, such as stop what you're doing, take medication, recover, and replenish.

Myth 2: Your brain reacts to events in the world. Your brain is not reacting to the world. It's predicting what will happen next. Your brain predicts what you need to do. Your brain is using patterns to determine what the body should do. Because the brain is working non-stop, 24/7 throughout your entire life, if your brain was only reacting to certain circumstances, this presumes that the brain is 'off' when it's not reacting, and this is not the case. In every moment, your brain uses all its available information — your memory, your situation, the state of your body — to make guesses about what will happen in the next moment. It tries to predict. Let's say you injured your foot, so you aren't able to run fast, that's even scarier if you're in danger, so there is an increase in the chemicals your body needs to run faster. Your brain is responsible for ensuring your body has what it needs to protect itself. This is also the reason why when adrenaline is spiked, it allows you to do things you normally wouldn't have done because the level of danger is predicted to be that high.

So, if we understand this, we understand the importance of consciously developing our brain with behavioral patterns that serve us well, not the ones that work against us. By reprogramming or rewiring our brain to understand a different pattern, we can eliminate unhealthy or harmful patterns or habits, such as negative self-talk or self-sabotage behavior. But you must first become aware of this pattern to reprogram or rewire your brain. The key to this is understanding that we need to do this consciously. Otherwise, the brain keeps predicting and it gets frustrated when it is conflicted and predicts incorrectly, squandering resources when they weren't warranted. This frustration causes stress levels to increase, confirming that your body effectuates the results of the brain.

The brain can be rewired; it can change. It's called neuroplasticity. Neuroplasticity refers to the brain's ability to form new connections and pathways and even change how its circuits are wired. For example, neurons with specific patterns can perform new tasks, changing the pathways in the brain. In the same way that the neurons that reside in what is called the ocular region are interpreting what we see, other neurons in other parts of the brain are also doing that job of interpreting what we're seeing. Neural pathways can change. But, regardless of which exact neuron is responsible, the more the pathway is used, the more the pattern is established. Your brain is busy managing what the body needs at all times. Your body has limited resources. In her book, Dr. Feldman Barret refers to as *body budgeting*- if the resources are depleted, your body can't perform at its best. This is why your brain becomes ineffective when you are sleep deprived. You will eventually crash because the brain needs to replenish its resources.

Myth 3: There is a clear dividing line between diseases of the body and mind. People think depression is a mental type of illness and that it has nothing to do with physical body diseases, such as cancer, heart disease, or diabetes.

This is not true.

In the seventeenth century, Rene Descartes, the founding father of modern medicine, was forced to sign a formal agreement with the Pope to obtain the human bodies he needed for dissection and research. The agreement imposed an absolute rule that he would only work with the physical realm; the mind, emotions, and soul were matters for the church This became known as Cartesian Duality and has dominated the practice of medicine for three centuries! As a result, some doctors will misdiagnose depression as a physical illness or anxiety as chest pain. The link between your soul hurting and your body hurting will become apparent in the coming chapters. In short, the body manifests what the brain and the soul feel. Recall that the brain is predicting and driving the action in your body.

Your brain follows a pattern of predicting and adapting. If someone loses their eyesight, the brain increases the predictions in the other senses; the ability to detect more nuances is heightened. An experiment was conducted where the subjects were blindfolded for a certain amount of time, and the brain, because it wasn't able to predict using the eyes, predicted based on other senses, so it amped up its ability to hear and assess from there.

The problem with doctors having the philosophy that the mind and the body are separate is that they misdiagnose emotion- or brain-related issues with body ailments because they are trained to treat the body. They treat the disease from a symptom perspective and not a cause perspective. Take blood pressure, for example. You may have high blood pressure, but you're so busy and so distracted that you're not even aware that something deep down is hurting; you're not paying attention to your own body, so you don't consciously sense it, but your brain does. Your brain identifies patterns and sees that something isn't working well, so it raises your blood pressure. A doctor will prescribe blood pressure medication, but you may not even need it. I was taking blood pressure medication for a while, and after I resolved a few issues, I was able to stop taking it. I changed nothing else other than consciously letting go of a troubling issue. When travel circumstances led me to miss my BP medication, I found myself feeling fine. I continued to test my theory for weeks by regularly checking it, and I could see it had returned to normal without using any medication.

Because the brain is trying to predict what you will need, it will continue using previously created patterns. The situation that initially created the pattern leads to what we experience as physiological symptoms. This specific situation needs to be explored, healed, and reprogrammed. The challenge is that it is not always easy to identify the origin of a pattern. It takes time. The work can be messy but crucial. Childhood trauma is an example of where the situation is likely not there anymore. However, the pattern will persist in the absence of reprogramming and healing. Humans constantly try to rationalize it away because our conscious selves use avoidance coping mechanisms.

Avoidance coping is a common maladaptation to hide from the pain in the short term without realizing that this is ineffective and will create more dysfunctional patterns. It is a dangerous and unsustainable mechanism. This is why many people often don't seek self-examination and mindful reflection as much as they should. They avoid it, try to sweep it under the carpet and deny that it's there, but that pattern will be there until it gets resolved. Some live their entire lives in misery because of this. It has also been found that many diseases originated due to this way of living. Much has been written about the connection between mind and body, citing research from the National Institute of Health (NIH)'s National Library of Medicine, confirming this is not just a theory. It references the field of psychoneuroimmunology, which has witnessed an explosion of empirical findings over the last two decades.

In particular, stress diminishes white blood cell response to viral infection and cancer cells.[6]

Links have been found between the mind and body in areas such as[7]

1. Heart disease and stroke are linked to panic disorder and depression.
2. Psoriasis is linked to depression.
3. Migraines are linked to anxiety, depression, and bipolar disorder.
4. Irritable bowel syndrome is linked to anxiety and depression.
5. Allergies and asthma are linked to depression.
6. Diabetes is linked to schizophrenia and depression.

The beautiful thing about our powerful brain is that addressing your mental struggles can prevent or significantly reduce these physical issues. Even better, once you learn how to manage them, they become less scary because you can see them for what it is, making it easier to work on and find closure. Because the brain tries to predict, it's always going to try to predict what's going to happen until it is resolved- negative or positive. *Will that guy call me back? Will I be able to get past this rejection that I've experienced? Will I be able to keep my job?*

---

6   https://pubmed.ncbi.nlm.nih.gov/18589562/
7   https://www.womenshealthmag.com/health/a18198138/
mind-body-connection-illnesses/

How well do you know yourself?

Socrates, the father of Western philosophy, said that, *Knowing thyself is the beginning of wisdom.* In modern times, Jay Shetty has reflected on this idea: *You can't possibly know what you want until you know who you are.* Both are profound to me because they are rooted in the same wisdom. You might think you want something, but if you don't know who you are, you may just like the idea of something even if that's not the best or right thing for you. I have found that people romanticize having, doing, or being something but are often misled for many reasons. For example, you might think you want a specific type of job, but you really only like the idea of the job, and it's not something you actually want to wake up and do every day of your life. Countless graduates with medical, legal, engineering, or other degrees discover that they are truly miserable in their jobs.

Do you love something, or do you love the idea of something?

Some people think, *I really want to be a movie star, I really want to be famous.* If you don't know yourself, you won't be able to answer the questions of whether you'll be able to handle what comes with that fame- the lack of privacy, the constant criticism and judgments on the way you look, the things you do, what you believe. Many people don't know what happens on all sides of what it takes to do specific jobs or live your life a certain way. Many people don't have the insight or self-reflection to think about what they actually want. I've coached clients who swore up and down that they wanted to take certain specific jobs or expand their business regionally and wanted guidance on the best way to get there. However, after applying my neuroscience-based assessment tool, they gained tremendous insights into their intrinsic behaviors and motivation drivers. They understood how they do what they do and why they do what they do. It uncovered blind spots and biases that have held them back or misled them. A guided focus on improving their metacognition empowered them with enhanced critical thinking skills and mindsets for making wiser decisions that significantly improved their confidence, opportunities, and overall happiness.

Client story – 'I've always wanted to [insert any example]' is a common theme I hear when working with clients. One client was an entrepreneur who aspired to expand his organization and be recognized as a leader in his space beyond the city where he operated. The phrase 'actions speak louder than words' continues to be true. The distinction is not as simple as that, however. Sometimes you are doing or not doing something because something else is in the way. Uncovering what that is may be one thing, but understanding the reason behind it is where true growth occurs. Not doing so is like putting a temporary patch on a punctured tire over and over again without repairing it. It is fraught with peril. With our exploratory work, he uncovered internal conflict and misalignment that were the source of an ongoing stress churn that started affecting his health. After successfully integrating the practice and development plan I designed for him, he no longer experienced the stress churn and improved his health.

Why does addressing these issues matter? The 2021 Gallup's State of the Global Workplace Report has unsettling findings of employee mental well-being.[8] The survey measured daily levels of engagement as well as the levels of daily stress, worry, sadness, and anger, each with increased percentage results compared to every year dating back to 2009. Experiences of worry occurred 41%, stress reached a record high of 43%, and anger also had a record high of 24%, primarily among employees younger than 40. Experiences of sadness increased by 4 points globally from 2019, with some regions seeing above-average daily sadness increases by 10 points from 2019.

I consistently find with my clients that their top-of-mind drive is for answers on what to do in certain situations they struggle with. It could be related to a job, a boss, colleague, spouse, family, neighbor, etc. In these cases, they only see part of the equation. They continue to be unhappy until they permit themselves to explore their role in the unfulfilling relationships. If you are not happy with yourself, you will likely not be happy anywhere you go.

---

8   https://www.gallup.com/workplace/349484/state-of-the-global-workplace.aspx

You have the power to turn that around. It's only a matter of learning how.

The decision-making challenges young adults face.

Based on what we know about the brain today, young adults face the challenge of choosing career paths when they have not yet reached full maturity. Schools and universities do not adequately prepare students for the complexities of the real world. Academic scores and accomplishments are not an indication of real-world performance. There is a lot of social pressure to 'know' what you want at this age and to make decisions accordingly. It becomes a difficult challenge to overcome, but it still needs to start with you.

A Microsoft survey validates that Gen Z was among the largest generation considering a career change due to their struggle in various aspects of work.[9]

	I struggle to bring new ideas to the table	I struggle to get a word in during meetings	I don't feel engaged or excited about work
Boomers	9%	9%	12%
Gen X	11%	11%	13%
Millennials	11%	12%	14%
Gen Z	14%	16%	16%

Getting to know yourself better, learning about who you are, and exercising your agency; these are skills our

---

9   https://ergonomictrends.com/great-resignation-statistics/

youth should be developing. When it comes time for our children to go to college and decide what they want to study, what we should do is make them aware that things change rapidly, and it's okay to choose something that they think they like, experiment, and change direction if they discover, *You know what, maybe this isn't really for me.* My main advice for young people is not to feel stuck- it's going to be okay because we continue to learn all the time. I'm doing what I thought I would never do, what I would say I would never do- teach and educate! We change our minds, and that's ok. The key is to avoid digging a deeper hole for yourself so that you change directions quickly.

When Albert Einstein was teaching at Princeton University in 1951, he had just administered an exam to an advanced class of physics students. On his way back to his office, his teaching assistant carried the set of completed exams. Despite his shyness, especially in the presence of the greatest physicist of the twentieth century, he asked him,

"Dr. Einstein, wasn't that the same exam you gave to this same group of students last year?"

Dr. Einstein thought for a second and said, "Yes, it was the same exam."

The assistant was now baffled and asked hesitantly, "But, Dr. Einstein, how could you give the same exam to the group of students, two years in a row?"

Einstein's answer was classic. He said, "Well, the answers have changed."

The point of this story was that the questions may have been the same but considering rapid developments and discoveries in the world of physics at that time, it was expected that the answers would be different than they might have been the prior year.

The power behind this story is that it applies to human perspectives on any subject or situation. There could very well be a time when you felt you had a masterful grasp of many areas of your life, career, goals, etc. You knew exactly where you stood; it felt fantastic, as if you were on top of the world! You had things figured out. As the world changes around us and we gain more and more experiences, many aspects of our lives change, and so do our beliefs, opinions, convictions, and even our values can change. We change as we grow, and that's okay.

Take parenthood, for example. I jokingly talk about the BC and AC periods: before children and after children. If you are in the BC period, your perspectives, priorities, and even values will change AC. Things you may never have understood or appreciated about your own upbringing now make more sense. No parent is perfect, but they will do their best and can only work with the raw materials they have. Therefore, it is incumbent upon every person to try, learn, and repeat. The wonderful thing about life is that it gives you agency, which provides you with two basic choices. You can build the habit of learning to improve upon, or you can reinforce learning to repeat the same mistakes. I placed my bets on the former.

It is during tumultuous times that genuinely knowing yourself is critical. Why? Because even in the best of times, blind spots and psychological biases are the proverbial monkey wrench of decision-making. When you add additional stress, decisions and actions can become irrational without realizing it in the heat of the moment. This is why there is such a thing as crimes of passion or legal defenses of temporary insanity. Even the acute stress alone could make you so weary and out of sorts that it is practically impossible to think clearly.

We are not born with a manual to teach us how to manage such disruptions effectively, yet we make roughly 35,000 decisions daily, on average. You would think we would've gotten really good at making decisions with so much practice. I've yet to meet a single person who has never asked themselves at one point or another, 'What was I thinking?!' Later in this book I explain in detail how we make decisions.

The passion disconnect

There is a myth that to be happy, you should know what your passion is and then pursue a career you are passionate about. But the fact is that we are delightfully complex beings, and we have many different passions, not just one. And as we gain more experiences in life, we develop more passions. The fallacy is that we can be passionate about something yet not have the skills or ability to fulfil it. That's just reality. Passion is sometimes confused with loving something or, as I mentioned earlier, liking the idea of something. The risk is when we don't know what we want, we bounce between different and often conflicting desires, like a dog chasing its tail. I see these trends worsening because we give away our agency and let others make that decision for us, like social media influencers, our typically unqualified family, friends, or other well-intentioned beings.

Self-concept

"A vision without action is just a dream. Action without a vision is a nightmare." - Joel Barker

The self-concept will make you or break you. Decades have proven this many times over – you will never rise above the level of your self-concept. My self-concept was that I would figure out how to break the chains of poverty. Therefore, I was an early student of Brian Tracy's 'The Psychology of Achievement.' How early? I have Tracy's program's complete cassette tape set I kept for posterity!

I never imagined that I would someday become certified as a Brian Tracy Business Coach. It was not in my plan. I wanted to use the best possible training to achieve my goals. I had a vision and was taking action to make it a reality. It started with learning the right strategy. I was immediately drawn to the psychology part because I was intrigued by how the mind worked. As an aside, despite my interest in it, I knew becoming a psychologist was not a profession that was high in demand or that would pay well. This was a driving force for me because I would not be a victim like my mother if I did what I needed to do to break those chains.

At that time, I was working full-time and taking some college courses at night. I distinctly remember driving from work to my class one night as I had a final exam and risking being late. I was so focused on getting there that I did not see the other car running the red light as I approached the intersection. It plowed into mine with accelerating force. I was not at fault, but I was visibly banged up. Limping with visibly torn pantyhose and scrapped legs to match, I was determined to get to class and take my exam. It was important to me. I explained to my professor why I was late. He had no trouble believing me just by looking at me! I completed the exam with flying colors. Thanks to Brian Tracy, I attributed my success to having total *clarity of purpose*, conquering obstacles, and not giving up.

So, what does this have to do with our perceived self-image? Pretty much everything because how people see themselves shapes their beliefs and value systems. Everyone has a self-concept or a set of identities from where beliefs form and take root. Our self-concept is the controlling factor of our performance, and we will perform consistently with it.

Write this down on a notepad, as it is important: The fact is, we cannot act in a manner inconsistent or contrary to our self-concept. Our self-concept precedes and predicts our levels of performance and effectiveness in everything we do.

The self-concept is a combination of ideas, thoughts, experiences, pictures, and things that have happened to us in our lives. Together, they form a composite image of the person we believe we are.

I should also mention that while we have a general concept of who we are, we also have hundreds of mini self-concepts or identities of who we are in various aspects of our lives. For example, we have a self-concept of how we are as a parent, boss, leader, spouse or partner, how we drive, how smart we are, how well we read, speak, present, negotiate, dress, etc. We will have a self-concept for each sport if we play multiple sports.

In each of these areas, our self-concept regulates how we perform in that area. Also, our overall self-concept is an average of all those mini self-concepts. The key to improving one's performance level is to increase your self-concept level because our brain can't perform at a higher level than the self-concept.

The more I exercised my focus and discipline on my goals, the more it strengthened my belief (therefore, my self-concept) that I would escape poverty. I gained the skills and perseverance to build a better future for myself at each turn. I had chosen to develop programming skills and eventually graduated with a Business and Information Technology degree from the University of Texas, Austin. My technical career took off in Silicon Valley's high-tech industry. I am living proof of my favorite quote:

"I am not a product of my circumstances. I am a product of my decisions." – Stephen R. Covey

Experiences that change you

As sure as death and taxes, there will be disruptions of all kinds in life. Life disruptions include family issues, moving, raising teens, getting married, becoming a parent, divorce, and bereavement. These are significant changes in our lives and often negatively impact our mental and physical health. No one escapes unscathed. To start with, sometimes these disruptions are unexpected, or you just didn't see it coming. But, even if you did see it coming, you have no idea what the impact will be until you experience it.

The other type of disruptions are business/career disruptions. This category ranges from making a work transition to shifts in the market, technologies, legal, or even competition shifts that disrupt your business or career.

Guess what? As we grow and develop, we're bound to experience many of these simultaneously, leading to significant changes in our worldview. The brain tries to predict to help you and your body do what you need to survive and thrive. However, experiences change your perspective by developing new patterns with the latest information. For example, you see things differently as a parent than before you have kids. Your worldview changes when you experience different countries and cultures than when you don't travel or relocate. The more experiences you have, the more you build mental fortitude, assuming you learned from the experience. If there is no lesson taken, there is no growth given. When there is no growth, the suffering is much higher.

Marcus Aurelius said, "We do not learn from experiences, we learn from reflection of experiences."

The COVID-19 pandemic is a perfect example of a disruption that amplified all other life disruptions and then some. The forced lockdowns, the lives lost, and epic levels of stress, anxiety, and uncertainty sent many spiraling from crises, challenges, and trauma. Mental health hotline calls surged to triple digits in some areas, and mental health landed front and center for employers like never before. Much is written about the negative impact of the pandemic, and the underlying fear remains as the hope of ever going back to 'normal' wanes. As a result, many began to take inventory and look at their lives from a new perspective that prompted the question, *Am I doing what I really want to be doing?* Some studies have shown that many people plan on quitting their jobs to go and do something else. The term associated with this mass exodus is 'The Great Resignation.' Initially, no one knew what the pandemic would mean for their lives. For many, the lockdown was the first time in years that some people had spent time with their families, rediscovering what's important to them.

In the biographical film, The Iron Lady, Meryl Streep portrays Margaret Thatcher, the longest-serving Prime Minister of the United Kingdom in the 20th century and the first woman to hold the office. Historical inaccuracies notwithstanding, she was aware that she had not mentally said goodbye to her beloved husband, whose ghost visits her. She conceals this from her doctor during her visits while also refusing further tests. She tells the doctor what her parents had taught her:

"Watch your thoughts for they become your words, watch your words for they become your actions, watch your actions for they become your habits, watch your habits for they become your character, watch your character for it becomes your destiny." She asserts, *"What we think, we become, and I think I'm fine."*

The lesson I extrapolate from this dialogue is that our brains create patterns driven by thoughts that, in turn, drive our responses, and the outcomes, good or bad, only reinforce the thought patterns. We cannot control much around us, but we must exercise our agency to control what we think, say, and do. It just takes clarity and conviction of purpose. It is easier said than done because life is full of disruptions that cloud our view and allow us to lose perspective. If disruptions occur around you, it is not your fault. But not learning and seeking clarity to deal with them is your fault.

The good news is that we possess the ability to create new, more productive patterns and replace ineffective ones. The ability to do so is called neuroplasticity. Neuroplasticity allows us to learn new things, enhance our cognitive capabilities, and even recover from strokes and traumatic brain injuries. It also allows our brains to move functions from one area of the brain to another if loss or decline occurs. More on this in later chapters.

Why our perception of ourselves is wrong

Illustration by T. Blackman[10]

Client story – Let's call her Sarah. Sarah came to me looking for help to position herself more strongly after getting laid off from a company over what she called a

10   cCegQ ABAA&cq=%27whoaa!+sorry+earl%2C+you+w-
      ere+in+my+blind+spot&gs_lcp=CgNpbWcQA1DBL1iXZGD-
      ndmgAcAB4AIABNlgBywGSAQE0mAEAoAEBqgELZ3dz-
      LXdpe 1pbWfAAQE&sclient=img&ei=Dvf1YdWqDZ7Y-
      0PEPuKO7sAw&bih=883&biw=1793&rlz=1C1RXMK_enU-
      S980LS981&hl=en-US#imgrc=w_piOwhiaBLAsM

technicality. Sarah had a technical background. We met as a result of a techie gathering I attended. She was anxious to discover any hidden talents that she could leverage. She agreed to do my assessment to see what she could discover. The behaviors section opens with three paragraphs summarizing the essence of how you do what you do, after which we break down the details. I ask her to read each statement and mark it as True, True with edit, or False. She hung on to her definition of each word, refusing to consider alternate meanings. She redlined and declared almost half of the statements False and most of the remainder True with an edit and a stark few as True, challenging everything from syntax to semantics and how it should be presented instead. When we arrived at the Perceptions section of the report, we saw a summary of her Self-Perception, Others' Perception – Moderate, and Others' Perception – Extreme. Moderate and Extreme relate when you are under moderate or extreme pressure, tension, stress, or fatigue. Descriptors in Others' Perception - Moderate included Pessimistic, Worrisome, Picky, and Fussy. Others' Perception – Extreme results included Perfectionist, Strict, Hard-to-Please, Defensive. While she agreed with her Self-Perception of being Moderate, Thorough, Knowledgeable, Diplomatic, and Analytical, she vehemently disagreed with the notion that others may perceive her as Picky, Fussy, Hard to Please, and Defensive.

*You can lead a horse to water, but
you can't force it to drink.*

There was a clear blind spot of a behavioral pattern and growth opportunity if she allowed it. It is not too different from an alcoholic who does not yet realize they are an alcoholic and that the first step to recovering is recognizing it. Nothing changes without the courage to examine yourself. If only she knew how much happier and more successful she would be if she were willing to be honest with herself. How empowered and unleashed she would feel.

We all have blind spots. We contradict ourselves without knowing it! I help my clients uncover different types of blind spots that are important to their companies and teams. These include strategic, cultural, human capital, and personal blind spots. These are our undetected and unexamined biases – the good, the bad, and the ugly.

A bias is not a preference – a preference presumes you have compared the selection options against each other. A bias is an inclination or predisposition without applying any comparison and, therefore, is void of impartial judgment. They cause or trigger predispositions to behave in a particular way/behavior. Biases are insidious and typically go undetected. For example, when hiring a new person for your team, leaders generally are inclined to hire someone who resembles them and the team. This led to the systemic lack of diversity in teams, companies, C-Suites, and boardrooms.

It is okay to be wrong - being wrong is par for the course and a normal part of the scientific process. As a highly analytical person with high standards, my singular focus has been uncovering the truth to arrive at the best solution. In projects, mediocrity or homogenization of ideas simply does not cut it. How delicious is a glass of milk when you have to add a variety of other liquids to it? This is how I used to see the concept of reaching a consensus that required everyone's idea be incorporated into the final product. It would merely dilute the solution and not meet the intended market needs.

I believed more in a divide-and-conquer model because we all have different talents and skills. Contrary to the majority of people, I personally love being wrong because when I am, I know I have learned something new and expanded my mind. It's a win for me. One of my managers at HP was likely the first one to put it in the right perspective for me. He said, "*Adriana, it is obvious that you end up being right 95% of the time in your analysis and recommendations. And you hold on with conviction when nobody else would see what you see.*"

Hard lesson: What could go wrong? It is easy to forget our impact on others when we're too focused on problem-solving. My savvy manager continued, "*As you push through, however, the result is a string of dead bodies in your wake. The downside is that the 5% of the time when you end up being wrong, you will be crucified.*" At that time, I could not see how my successes could hurt me because of the way I justified them in my mind. For me, it was all about the greater good, and I never realized others would resent me.

I found it challenging to understand this concept decades ago because if someone had a better case and could defend it, I was all in and would champion it. Furthermore, I appreciated learning something new that I had not thought about. Looking back, I now know where my biases and blind spots were. If I had developed my emotional intelligence back then, I still would've accomplished my success rate without the string of dead bodies.

In scientific research, being wrong is part of the process, and it is well-established that being wrong leads to more learning. Scientists embrace the possibility of being wrong. They do their best with the tools they have until new tools extend opportunities to examine more deeply, broadly, or precisely. Over time, new discoveries lead us to major course corrections in our understanding of how the world works, such as natural selection and quantum physics.

Our perception of ourselves is also wrong because we don't take time to practice internal reflection, examine a recent interaction or series of events, and look for patterns, signs of emotions experienced at that time or observed in others. You can become comfortably numb and not even realize it. You get 'used to' the pain and either settle or give in to acceptance. The problem is that it is still there, eating away at you. Metaphorically, you don't know whether your house has termites unless you are looking for them. You'd know if you have a termite inspector who knows exactly how to look for signs and where to look for them. They will determine the extent of the damage and propose a solution.

The termites are like the unresolved pain that stays there, eating away at you throughout your life, subversively eroding your soul and ability to function as your optimal self in the same way the termites can destroy your house if left unattended. This pain can take several forms- guilt, shame, humiliation, embarrassment, and remorse, just to name a few.

Guilt and shame are the most painful of human emotions. If you have not yet seen Brene Brown's TED Talk, I highly recommend you watch it.[11] Worse, guilt and shame can lead to depression, anxiety, paranoia, and other mental health disorders.

Imagine what would happen if you were buying a house and waived having it inspected by a professional? I can't imagine anyone would. So, why do people make so many important decisions without checking for bias or blind spots to avert bad choices?

---

11   https://www.ted.com/talks/brene_brown_the_power_of_vulner-ability?language=en

You need to self-disrupt before you self-destruct. Only then will you be able to move into a powerful position and enhance all aspects of your life. It requires courage to take a much closer look at oneself. Your desire for change needs to be stronger than your desire to remain the same. This is called intrinsic motivation. You can use the resource at the end of this chapter to further understand and explore your internal mental landscape.

Resources

The Metacognitive Awareness Inventory is an instrument designed to assess general self-regulated learning skills across the disciplines. *"The Secret of Self-Regulated Learning."* Faculty Focus.[12]

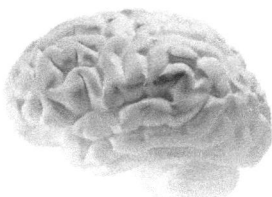

CHAPTER 2

THE NEUROSCIENCE OF FEAR:

"You must do the thing you think you cannot do." – Eleanor Roosevelt

In 2020, millions faced the brutal realization that nobody was safe and that not everyone could be saved. A deadly pandemic swept the world and literally and metaphorically brought everyone to their knees. This was a harsh new reality and a huge contributor to what I called Coronavirus PTSD. I anticipated its impact in December 2019, well before the mass shutdowns began in the US in March 2020, two months after the first US case of COVID-19 appeared in January.

What is Coronavirus PTSD?

PTSD is the acronym for Post-Traumatic Stress Disorder. The American Psychiatric Association defines PTSD as a psychiatric disorder that may occur in people who have experienced or witnessed a traumatic event such as a natural disaster, a severe accident, a terrorist act, war/

combat, rape, or people who have been threatened with death, sexual violence, or serious injury.[13]

I coined the term Coronavirus PTSD because it specifically relates to the life-or-death threat of the pandemic while having no ability to control it. Among the most brutally hit were the frontline healthcare professionals. The toll of witnessing so much death was unbearable for some, who committed suicide to stop the pain. Others constantly feared for their safety and what they might bring home to their families after work. The mental health symptoms parallel those seen in other trauma that results in PTSD, such as war, where your life is constantly in danger, child abuse or sexual abuse, and other life-threatening events where you have no control and cannot help yourself. Based on the spread in China, I saw the same parallels right from the beginning.

While I'm not a clinician to provide a diagnosis, my goal was to help as many people as possible deal with anxiety, fear, stress, and uncertainty. I created this basic set of questions to help shed light on the type of care they needed the most.

---

13   https://www.psychiatry.org/patients-families/ptsd/what-is-ptsd

The signs of Coronavirus PTSD

1. Have you witnessed or experienced a life-threatening event?
2. Do you avoid activities, people, or thoughts related to the event?
3. Do you have trouble getting the event off your mind?
4. Do you feel intensely afraid, horrified, or helpless?
5. Do you have trouble functioning the way you used to?
6. Do you have trouble sleeping?

If they answered yes to two or more of these questions, they may be experiencing Coronavirus PTSD, indicating that they should seek medical help and get this addressed. These symptoms are natural responses for people forced into isolation but are worsened by the constant influx of news reminding them of the horror and their inability to escape it. From what I have studied, there are varying degrees of trauma, and the impact is different for people at different developmental stages.

But there *is* good news, which is why I wrote this book. There are ways to rewire your brain because your brain will function based on patterns developed throughout your life. Those patterns culminate experiences and the emotions associated with those experiences. But as you grow and you add more experiences to your life, you will eventually have more experiences that will change that previous experience from being the driving force in your life. If you don't repeat the trauma, you can learn to feel safe again and to function normally through additional reinforcing experiences and environments that you can create for yourself.

Depending on how young you are when experiencing the trauma, you may not forget it but adapt to it; it doesn't have to dominate your outlook and performance. How long the PTSD lasts depends on the treatment you receive and the environments you create around you. Experiences are a part of you because you had that experience. The brain is always predicting, so when you bring a memory or experience to the forefront, your brain will predict what the body needs, and if it's a fear experience, it will raise your cortisol level and trigger your fight or flight readiness. Your brain does not decipher the context; it looks at what you are seeing consciously, whether you are observing it and it's happening in real-time or whether it's a memory and you are reliving it. Retrieved emotions from that experience are triggered, and your brain says, *Oh, we're going to need more of this*, and it prepares your body to take the action that it would need physically. We experience these physiological reactions as fear, anxiety, or panic because we have come to associate the physical with the emotional.

Fear is contagious. Let's say you see people running away from something- you're going to feel fear. You don't yet know why, but you start running, too. Our internal senses identify that people look scared, so our brain tries to predict what the body needs to survive this situation. It raises our bodily reactions and all the necessary chemicals to get into action. The danger is that it takes away from your thinking and goes more into reacting- being ready to run. Because the brain balances resources, instead of putting those resources into planning or something that would have otherwise gotten your attention, it's putting them into, *"You better get ready to run because there is something that appears scary."* Mammals are wired in very similar ways. If one antelope starts running, the others will start running because they know something is wrong.

Webster's dictionary defines fear as a feeling you become aware of, either directly or indirectly, such as through other people, that you expect something unpleasant to happen. In the case of Coronavirus, we would hear what was happening and think, *Ok, this could happen to me, too.*

Neuroscientist Joseph LeDoux focused his research on survival circuits and their impact on emotions such as fear and anxiety. The circuits are there, and they will definitely take action when there is danger or a threat. This is how the brain keeps the body safe, because the body's survival depends on it – the brain's number two job after body budgeting. He shares a similar theory to Dr. Lisa Feldman Barret in her approach to the emotion of fear in that we construct it; it's not already there, taking an exact form; we construct it every single time. Part of what

we use to construct that emotion is previous experiences-
any patterns or our physical state at the time. For example,
I'm usually relatively fearless and steady during
emergencies. HOWEVER, when I was eight months
pregnant and out for a walk with my husband, we passed
a house and suddenly heard a dog rushing to the fence
and barking aggressively. I was very aware that I was on
the sidewalk and that there was a fence keeping the dog
in. Still, just the idea that the dog was getting closer to me,
knowing that I would not be able to run or protect myself
and my baby, terrified me as I felt physically vulnerable.
We construct the fear emotion according to our body
state and all the information we have at that time. The
brain predicts what you will need and how well you can
survive. It will feed your body to ready it and take away
from other processes if need be.

During the pandemic, medical
professionals and frontline
workers exposed to people
dying daily have been through
Coronavirus PTSD. The rate of
suicide for doctors increased
during the pandemic because
the constant death was too
brutal to tolerate. There was a
New York paramedic who said, '*I'm terrified of what I've
already possibly brought home.*' The unknown feeds a
state of uncertainty, and uncertainty feeds anxiety. When
uncertainty is the only certainty, you will have escalating

anxiety. Anxiety is what carries the seed of fear. So, the higher the uncertainty, the higher the fear.

I hope this book gives you, the reader, information and a positive way to clarify how fear and other emotions are created and that it's a normal and human emotion.

Key Point: Fear is there but doesn't need to control you. The fear emotion lies to your soul and robs you of your courage before it is even born. But there is a way out. If you can learn to become a witness to the experience of fear in your mind, you can separate yourself from it and gain control over it. People who do not understand this allow fear to prevent them from getting the help they need because of the stigma that still permeates our society regarding mental health.

I first read the book *Think and Grow Rich* by Napolean Hill in 1979.[14] I was effectively homeless at the time and couch-surfing until I could get back on my feet. The book became instrumental in me turning the corner. It helped me build my ability to deal with my fears and the courage and strength to go after what I wanted to break away from the poverty cycle. In his book, Hill describes six different kinds of fear that carry the power to either hold us back from what we want and deserve or ultimately destroy us if we let them. Nothing beats facing your fears head-on. It is tremendously empowering. And it comes down to only two choices – love or fear. Choose love, starting

---

14   Hill, Napolean. Think and Grow Rich. 1937.

with yourself. Don't let fear turn you against your playful heart. In my case, I didn't have the luxury of a playful heart because it was more about survival, determination, and discipline. I didn't choose fear because what I feared most was staying stuck in the mindset and poverty cycle like my mom. My desire to change was far stronger than my desire to remain the same.

Uncovering and unveiling six basic fears

1. **Fear of poverty.** I feared poverty because I knew how miserable my mother had been, and I did not want to grow up like her- without education, opportunities, or a loving life partner. My mom raised us all by herself on welfare and food stamps. I had three brothers, and I was third in line. This impacted my life in so many ways. As a child, I was a victim of my circumstances because I had no power. I was a victim of being born into a set of cultural, economic, and ignorant environmental forces. My mom was not nurturing or supportive; she barely kept her head above water, trying to raise us alone, so she was stuck and helpless. Despite that, I'm grateful she never abandoned us and did the best she could despite her damaged soul and limited intellectual capacity. To her credit, she also kept us on the straight and narrow, forbidding us from hanging around with the rotten apples or gangs in the hood. None of us ever got arrested or tried drugs. My father chose

to be absent instead of taking responsibility for providing support of any kind to his children.

Culture dictated that as the only girl, I was the one who was supposed to stay and take care of her like my aunt Elisa did for her parents. As such, she would harass me when I was trying to study. She grew up being told that girls don't need to study. They needed to learn how to keep house, wash, and do everything to be worthy of a good man. These teachings only served to develop a deep-seated, fear-based response in her, further entrenching psychological and cultural biases.

2. **Fear of criticism.** My grandmother was not nurturing at all. She was full of criticism and dished it out to no end. Grandma was horrible; she would tell me, *You're ugly and dirty! Get away from here!* So, of course, my mom carried on in the same way – constantly criticizing and shaming us. When you come from a negative situation that has created dysfunctional patterns, these patterns and experiences become direct ingredients to your beliefs, and those beliefs are the ingredients that make up your self-concept. When there is so much reinforcement of these negative beliefs, your self-concept can never elevate, which means you can't rise above them. When you try to learn something new, you will never perform higher than your self-concept. You can't. This point is so

fundamentally important that it is worth repeating in the context of this fear.

The stronger your self-concept, the better you'll be able to perform. I'm sure you're asking yourself: *If that is the case, and with all the negativity I grew up with, why did I perform?* Remember what I said before? Your willingness to change has to be stronger than your willingness to stay the same. It was one of the driving forces behind my performance.

I mentioned entering the workforce full-time at fourteen and never stopped working. I took great pleasure in that because I was gaining life experiences. I had an unquenchable thirst to learn anything and everything that would help me improve my odds of moving up in the world. I was ambitious and determined. I truly believe that entrepreneurs are willing to do things nobody else would consider doing *to achieve their goals.* I succeeded in my goal to ensure my education. I was the first person in my family to graduate with a degree from a major university. Before graduation, I secured a computer engineering job in California and left Texas.

Despite my accomplishments, dealing with my inferiority complex took a long time. While I'm an extrovert, I built a wall around myself to avoid the fear and shame of anyone possibly discovering how I grew up. Imposter syndrome, much? Later, I learned that the wall only kept me from having many more meaningful, trusting relationships. I didn't mind it then because I didn't grow up with trusting and meaningful relationships, so I didn't know what I was missing. I was simultaneously lucky and unlucky. All I knew was that fears will persist unless you work on facing them. If you don't face them down, they'll face you down and prevent you from growing.

Not having a dependable father made it hard to consider trusting romantic relationships, so I remained fiercely independent. While this made me very self-sufficient and resourceful and allowed me to lift myself out of poverty, having meaningful relationships was complicated. I also believed that I couldn't trust men. During my teen working years, I witnessed many married male co-workers in Texas having girlfriends on the side. Not to mention my mom's experience; I was not about to allow that. It took me a long time to let go of that fear and fully trust my husband of thirty years. Thank God he was patient!

If I had the training and understanding of emotional intelligence I have now back then, it would have given me a significant advantage. No doubt, I would've avoided many hard lessons and unwise decisions along the way because of this fear.

3. **Fear of ill health** is often associated with the fear of old age and death. The idea of losing your physiological abilities is scary, and experiments have proved that people can be made ill by suggestion. Here's the neuroscience behind it:

    ■ Research has shown two sides to the power of suggestion – the placebo effect and the nocebo effect. The placebo effect will make you well even if you only receive a sugar pill. The nocebo effect can make you ill if you believe the side effects are terrible, even when you take a placebo. People can make themselves or others sick through suggestions and beliefs, often diagnosed as hypochondria.

    ■ The seed of this fear lives in human minds. Take, for example, the suicides of competitive athletes who tragically succumb to disease or severe injury that robs them of their abilities, hopes, and dreams.

    ■ The power of the mind is limitless: it can build or it can destroy. There are many uplifting examples of people who persevere despite their disabilities. Take paraplegic skateboarder Evan Lalanne, the world's fastest blind Olympic runner, David Brown, or Australian motivational speaker Nick Vujicic, born with no legs and no arms. You can yield to or rise above fear; both powers lie within you.

I've always marveled at elders who can impart their wisdom with love and care despite ill health. I enjoy having conversations about life's trials and tribulations. You will learn from their lessons if you can set your ego aside. It is also an opportunity to establish a mindset of what kind of person you want to be when you become an elder. I saw a video interview of several eighty-somethings with questions about happiness, regrets, challenges, and what they would change if they could. The resulting article was *"Eightysomethings: A Practical Guide to Letting Go, Aging Well, and Finding Unexpected Happiness,"* by Katharine Esty, Ph.D. She said, *"After interviewing many other eightysomethings who were less healthy, I discerned that people fall into five main groups according to how they cope with their health issues. Deniers, Stoics, Complainers, Worriers, and Realists. The coping style does not seem related to the severity of their health problems."* [15] This is a crucial point to keep in mind.

---

15 From article citing Excerpted with permission from "Eightysome-things: A Practical Guide to Letting Go, Aging Well, and Finding Unexpected Happiness" by Katharine Esty, PhD. Copyright 2019 by Skyhorse Publishing, Inc.) article link https://www.salon.com/2019/09/15/i-interviewed-people-in-their-80s-about-how-they-cope-with-aging-heres-what-i-learned/

4. **Fear of loss of love or someone.** As mammals, we are social creatures and, as such, need other humans. There is also a biological need for a love connection for companionship or procreation. However, if we don't feel sufficient in ourselves, the distress of losing someone's love manifests itself as fear giving way to do anything to avoid this fear.

Fear avoidance only leads to more unhappiness. For example, some people will stay in unsatisfying or dysfunctional relationships because they fear they need someone to fill a void or make them whole. They may also believe they cannot be responsible for themselves and may use the person as a crutch. The maladaptive thinking is that they don't fundamentally accept they're good enough or capable enough. This thinking is a lie born out of unhealthy patterns in your brain, most likely rooted in early childhood experiences. This is your brain working against you, not for you. If you can love yourself for who you are, you don't *need* (and 'need' is the key word here) another person. Do you *want* another person? Perhaps, but you don't need them to feel complete. We are designed to function in relationships with other human beings, but you have a say in the type of relationship you choose. We aren't intended for isolation, which is why the Coronavirus pandemic was traumatizing for so many people. Fostering healthy relationships will help you meet this need for connection without sacrificing your sense of self.

5. **Fear of old age**. In addition to facing the fear of ill health, the fear of old age is commonly tied to eroticism through diminished sexual attraction from others. Additional causes of this fear include loss of freedom and independence brought upon losing physical and economic freedom. The neuroscience of it:

   - Typically, as people age, they may slow down and feel afraid. As it persists, it becomes a phobia called gerascophobia.
   - The fear can develop into an inferiority complex, telling themselves they are 'slipping' because of age.
   - Based on this fear, they lose initiative, imagination, and self-reliance, often born from a depressive state.
   - It often triggers anxiety related to money, self-sustainability, deteriorating health, being unable to live at home, manage daily tasks of living, feeling alone or isolated, and falling or getting injured,

We tell ourselves that story instead of looking from the perspective of this simple fact: some of the most valuable years, mentally and spiritually, are those in later life. Clinical mental impairment diseases notwithstanding, a person will possess a wealth of information, wisdom, lessons learned, and memories to cherish and celebrate.

While these are valid concerns, at the same time, age is a fact of life. Aging gracefully means you accept where you are, and remembering the days when you were young and fearless makes you smile. You can appreciate what you have now that you didn't have back then, like more wisdom and experience. Focusing on what you are losing is not healthy for your self-concept and beliefs. If you believe you can only be happy if you could be younger and pain-free, that's putting your whole self-concept into something you have no control over. Instead of living for the now and the future, you're living for the past that once was.

If you're fearful of old age and losing some capacity, examining why that fear is there is advisable. Where is it coming from? How you feel about something will affect your self-concept and beliefs, driving your ability to enjoy life at any age. It also impacts your current quality of life. Perhaps you decide to go after a new career or try a new hobby you always wanted to try. It is never too late. Think of Harland Sanders, who, up until age 50, had been a farmer, fireman, insurance salesman, and streetcar conductor. At age 62, he franchised

Kentucky Fried Chicken. Duncan Hines (his brand and real name) didn't discover his culinary career until he was 55. People like Ronald Reagan and Arnold Schwarzenegger left Hollywood for Politics at 54 and 56 respectively. You can give yourself another chance. In effect, you guarantee your failure simply by not trying.

6. Fear of death

Hill says, *"This fear is simultaneously the cruellest, most useless of the six fears"* because everyone is going to die! You can't avoid it. Humans live longer now than ever before. If you're worried about dying when you turn sixty, know that some people are already in their fourth career. I have a friend who always says, *"We're not here for a long time. We're here for a good time!"* The attitudes you develop will shape the beliefs that will get you through this or sink you into misery until you die.

What do you fear? Let's now put it in perspective. During the pandemic, people mistook PTSD for stress and suffered significantly more by not understanding the difference. Fear is part of being human and necessary for survival, but it needs to be. Try this framework for assessing fear and maintaining perspective.

The Three Levels of Fear

Fear Level 1: Fear at a distance. You hear about a hurricane three or four states away. You see it, and you say, *Wow, that's scary.* You acknowledge it. Avoid internalizing it because it is outside your control.

Fear Level 2: Fear in your neighborhood. The hurricane is in your state. There's a possibility that it could move closer to you, but you don't really know. You are in an alert state. This is a good time to check your preparedness level and make a plan, just in case.

Fear Level 3: Fear on your doorstep. The hurricane is upon you, and if you've not been taking measures to stay safe by now for whatever reason, your fear is going to get out of control.

When the pandemic was announced, and it started to spread to other countries in Asia and Europe, we knew it was a matter of time before it reached the U.S. During the 2019 holidays, my daughter and son came home from Seattle, Washington. We were all having a great time celebrating Christmas together. We knew about COVID, and that was our **Fear Level 1**, because it was apparent that *It was spreading, and it was spreading fast.* We cautioned them to stay vigilant.

Then, when the first U.S. case hit the Seattle area in January 2020, it brought about fear **Fear Level 2**. There were no such things as lockdowns and travel restrictions during this time. At **Fear Level 2**, my husband and I started taking action, stockpiling water and certain groceries and staples, because we understood the pattern. We didn't wait until it was at our doorstep. That day was March 6, 2020, when the first COVID case hit our county, bringing about **Fear Level 3**. Most people were unprepared and panicked when the news stations began reporting the rush at grocery stores. No one could have imagined such a thing as empty grocery shelves and the war for toilet paper!

We were prepared with supplies but still had to take the utmost precautions because my mother-in-law, who lives with us, has COPD (Chronic Obstructive Pulmonary Disease) and needs oxygen 24/7. She also has other underlying conditions and would likely not survive COVID. We maintained the highest safety protocols but managed our fear by reducing the risk because we took action ahead of the panic.

The lesson here is to be as aware as you can and put the fear into perspective based on proximity. Don't wait until Level 3 to take the appropriate actions to mitigate the situation and decrease the negative impact. Don't let fear control you; have a little bit of faith, and if you are paying attention and preparing, you will likely be okay-your losses will be minimized. No matter how bad it gets, remember that:

You have survived every single thing that you thought you wouldn't.

Managing During Turbulent Times- For Leaders

We often forget that different people have different circumstances, family histories, and experiences, creating different reactions with varying manifestations during turbulent times. This is a staunch reminder to all managers and leaders that we all manage things differently and react differently to situations, so we must avoid presuming what will and will not serve to *relieve everyone's fear*. Just because it eases your worries, it doesn't mean it will reduce others worries.

If you are a business owner or run a business, the prevailing question during turbulence is, 'How will my business survive these turbulent times?' As leaders, I suggest that business owners ask themselves other, more critical questions.

Exercise:

Step 1: Answer these five questions below. Give them thought and answer honestly.

1. How do I show up during a crisis?
2. How adaptable am I?
3. Do I foster a learning culture?
4. Have I examined my Knowing-Doing Gap - where my actions don't coincide with what I know I should do?
5. Do I trust my team, and does my team trust me?

Step 2: Ask five people who know you well or work with you to answer these questions about you. Write them down. The only rule: Say nothing in response except for these words, *"Thank you for telling me the truth about what I needed to hear."*

These are incredibly tough questions that every leader should ask themselves, not only during a crisis but in general. When you see a situation coming, you should already understand these things about yourself. This is how you avoid repeating past mistakes you later regret.

Why is this so important? The faster change happens, the higher the uncertainty. As leaders, we need to become comfortable with that because CEOs today are expected to have more breadth and depth about things they never had to do or know before. The pace and the magnitude of disruptive changes have forced this trend. I've tracked the list of leaders' top ten concerns change for years and it is clear that leaders become more reactive and less strategic. The previous year's top ten did not go away. They merely ranked lower because of new, higher pain points. As a result, leaders become reactive. Here are a few examples I've compiled from six years of annual reports of leadership challenges from surveying 1,453 board members and C-suite executives worldwide annual report by the North Carolina State University's ERM initiative together with Protiviti.

LEADERSHIP CHALLENGES RANKING	2023	2022	2021	2020	2019	2018
Succession challenges - ability to attract & retain talent limits ability to achieve operational targets	1	2	8	3	2	6
Economic conditions restrict growth and margins - requires new skill sets	2	5	2	2	N/A	N/A
Resistance to change in our culture may restrict making timely necessary adjustments to the business model and operations	4	7	9	5	5	N/A
The adoption of new technologies may require new skills in short supply requiring significant efforts to reskill/upskill existing employees.	7	4	4	10	N/A	N/A
Our organization's culture may not timely identify escalation of risks and market opportunities	8	N/A	N/A	8	9	5
Our approach to managing ongoing demands and expectations may negatively impact our ability to retain talent and our effectiveness and efficiency	9	N/A	N/A	N/A	N/A	N/A
Our organization may not be sufficiently resilient and/or agile to manage unexpected crisis - impacting operations and reputation	10	N/A	N/A	N/A	N/A	N/A

Dominating the top ten for 2023 are culture and people concerns. It is no surprise given that many CEOs have not built a higher tolerance for ambiguity and agility in decision-making skills, which means building a more agile mind to predict things faster and make better decisions. They need to have the ability to develop and maintain a high-quality team, and that requires more attention than just giving perks. Multiple reports indicate that employees would prefer going to a competitor, even if they earned a little bit less, if the competitor had a better culture. CEOs would know this if they were paying attention, but they are too distracted. Right now, the workforce demands transparency, diversity, equity, and inclusion - things that have nothing to do with snacks, Kombucha, and napping pods.

Today, it is essential for CEOs to upskill in communication and their ability to inspire employees. A survey of 200 CEOs and Boards of Directors cited communication skills among the top five missing skills that impacted the bottom line. I've seen many who suffer from a severe lack of emotional intelligence and cannot see beyond their blind spots and biases to recognize the problem. Leaders often avoid this because they are scared, and they are right. It is scary. It requires true strength and courage to do this work, but the ROI makes it worth it. Having an agile mind is critically important because your success and your company's future rests on keeping your blind spots in check, addressing your unexamined assumptions and biases, and taking the appropriate actions quickly. This is how you must fortify yourself before managing during any crisis.

Remember this: businesses have a value chain- one thing triggers another. Fear also has its value chain. It starts with a particular event. When the event is not clear or well understood, uncertainty grows. In the inability to resolve the uncertainty, tension builds, which feeds anxiety. As your environment presents real or perceived threats, a sense of powerlessness creeps in and feeds fear. One catalyzes the other, creating the lifecycle of fear.

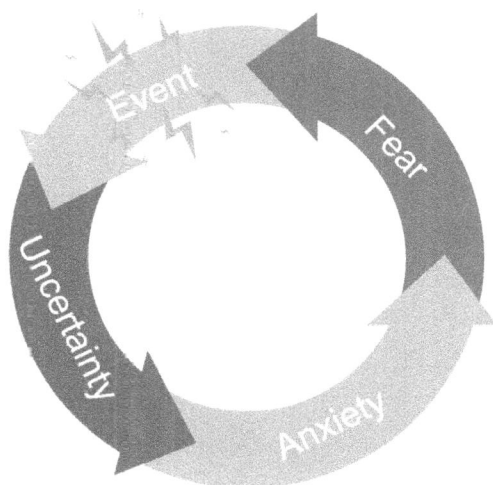

The Lifecycle of Fear

Trackback: What is the root cause of your fear? This type of self-discovery can lead to productive strategies that will reduce unnecessary anxiety and successfully navigate uncertainty.

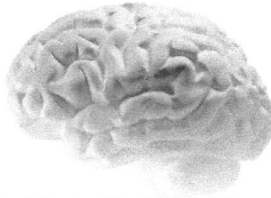

CHAPTER 3

THE LIMITATIONS OF THE GROWTH MINDSET

"If management stopped demotivating their employees, then they wouldn't have to worry so much about motivating them." W. Edwards Stemming.

As part of my consulting projects and continuous learning efforts, staying on top of the latest approaches to building success and managing teams has always been important. One of the approaches that grabbed my attention years ago and, from my observations, felt like it took off like wildfire was a book by Carol Dweck titled *Growth Mindset* published in 2006. As Dweck summarizes, individuals who believe their talents can be developed (through hard work, good strategies, and input from others) have a growth mindset. They tend to achieve more than those with a more fixed mindset (those who believe their talents are innate gifts).

I explored it by attending many courses and webinars containing Dweck's growth mindset theory. I found a variety of interpretations and explanations of it as they applied it to different points or issues. In particular, I remember one presentation that cleverly positioned Growth Mindset to encourage a culture of risk by distinguishing smart risks and dumb risks. It promoted that a growth mindset would enable companies to discover new opportunities by taking risks.

I felt the authors aligned with my observations in large enterprise companies. The trend for established companies was getting more and more risk averse. Established companies became comfortable attracting customers with brand name recognition without the need to hunt for their next meal. This was fine during the 60s, 70s, and 80s because technologies were not moving as fast as today. Also, at that time, people would stay in the same job for a long time, even for a lifetime. I instinctively felt this would not be sustainable because things change, and I have routinely observed those changes. Besides, it was in my nature to remain hungry and keep hunting.

With that perspective, I looked at the concept of a growth mindset similarly. It required taking smart risks to grow. Corporate America jumped on the growth mindset bandwagon as it was such a hot topic. All the managers said, '*We're going to have a growth mindset in this organization.*' Ultimately, the term gets tossed around so much that it loses its effect. Mainly because using the term doesn't mean you understand its true essence. In 2019, I was already at the point where I was going to write an article specifically on Growth Mindset, and I thought I would title it, *When Growth Mindset goes bad!* I thought I'd start by researching and seeing where and how it had been going. I was already critical of how some companies had implemented it. I interviewed and talked to other leaders and CEOs during a time I had spent evaluating educational pedagogies. I gathered that the notion of a growth mindset was not as successful as they perceived it to be. I'm using the word perceived because as I started looking into it, my experience was contrary to the teachings and webinars that were going on. I then came across an article from 2017 that had publicly called out the problems with the growth mindset theory. This article, published by TES Committee, criticized the growth mindset concept as, *'All hype and no benefit.'* I learned that several issues cited by this committee claimed that the growth mindset wasn't meeting expectations. In particular it stated that "...*what Carol Dweck was offering was the equivalent to Brain Gym or other learning styles that came before it that didn't produce the results that you would think.*"[16]

Here's the point: What does it tell you when you observe that almost everyone who talks about Growth Mindset hasn't even read Carol Dweck's research? This falls into the same instant gratification behavior patterns that I noticed, where people seek a quick fix while ignoring or

---

16   https://www.tes.com/news/growth-mindset-where-did-it-go-wrong)

misunderstanding the real intent and the actual usage of a scientific theory.

"This book, Growth Mindset, is by far the most unread book in educational dialogue and the most widely discussed."17

In my opinion, this is not irony- it is hypocrisy. There is a growing trend to fall back on an instant gratification culture that expects some magic fix, and they're willing to bastardize detailed work instead of examining it. They don't consider understanding the underlying systems impacted or assess the potential damage caused by its misuse. Instead, they blame the researcher for not solving the problem they believe should have been solved, and that's unfortunate. The real reason behind Dweck's research was to improve IQ by inspiring kids to be challengers and independent thinkers. It was not to get kids to behave or get higher mathematics scores. The work of teaching and learning is still required.

I applaud all efforts that support creating the next generation of critical thinkers and innovators - that's near and dear to my heart. My previous business, NanoTecNexus Inc., focused on nanotechnology in industry and academic scientific research. My passion later led me to start a sister company called NanoTecNexus Learning Group

---

17 https://www.tes.com/magazine/archive/weekend-read-growth-mindset-new-learning-styles

(NLG). NLG was explicitly focused on K-12 to inspire the next generation of innovators and inventors by getting them interested in STEM education-Science, Technology, Engineering, and Mathematics. I incorporated Dweck's Growth Mindset theory into our education programs to inspire learning.

Organizational Arthritis

As in other past business and management concepts, I observed a misuse and misapplication of the Growth Mindset theory in the workplace. The unintended misuse led to the creation of internal social groups rallying around the term while often excluding those who would buck groupthink by truly applying a growth mindset and being innovative and independent thinkers. Think about this: a growth mindset must be developed internally and requires practice. It's not about calling out others you believe are not practicing a growth mindset simply because they don't think the same things you do. It's a common trap for most people. Companies benefit if employees think beyond their current restraints, yet they do not encourage Socratic discourse. The intention to promote the concept of a growth mindset is there, but the application gets completely marginalized. Recognizing this requires a lot of presence, critical observation and thinking, and exploration. We don't often have the opportunity, ability, or incentive to dive deeper into our thoughts and ways of being. Because of the patterns within our society of wanting a quick fix, it is incumbent on every single individual to make the growth mindset work for them.

From a scientific and research perspective, there will always be more work and experiments to be conducted on any topic, resulting in new findings to publish. The researchers are not responsible for implementing the findings; however, they want to receive feedback from people to determine whether the findings worked on a practical level, how well they worked, and if they didn't, why. I feel for Carol Dweck because she was chastised for presumably not solving a problem. It mattered not that the Growth Mindset was presented as a theory and not a solution. When she tried to explain that perhaps the implementation was wrong and wanted to learn more about how the Growth Mindset had been applied in various situations, she was cast as being defensive. And that's not the case at all. She was not being defensive; as a researcher, she naturally wanted more data. This is where nuances on improper implementation start to appear.

That article highlighted what I had observed long before Dweck's book was published. There are patterns and biases- mental models- within which people get stuck. Mental models are part of how the brain makes sense of the vast amount of information it processes every moment of every day. They are the framework and lens through which we see the world. Unlike biases, they filter the signal from noise and attribute cause and effect—the "sorting hat" to decide what makes it into our conscious awareness.

I've encountered hundreds of mental models across different industries, professions, functions, and purposes. I've curated the best of the best mental models to use when working with private clients to empower them with the right tools and techniques that work best for their situation, background, and profession and prevent them from getting stuck. Once stuck in this limited thinking, people tend to stay stuck and lose their mental agility, as arthritis does to joints. The antidote for this is a deliberate and focused practice to develop a growth mindset and emotional intelligence. Increasing your self-awareness and practicing daily reflection is a great way to start. When I work with clients, we accomplish this in the first six weeks as part of the discovery phase of my programs. It's the beginning of powerful and positive transformations.

It opens the gateway to adopt something new without expecting quick returns or merely hand-waving systemic problems such as diversity, equality, and equity. Without mental flexibility, people can't adapt to new mental models. This problem exists and is baked into leadership in large and small companies. In large corporations with matrix organizations, teams are located worldwide in different departments and divisions, yet they are all collaborating. While that sometimes sounds progressive and exciting, it can also be very frustrating when getting things done.

Organizational arthritis has been around for a long time, evidenced by companies that did not adapt to new trends – IBM did not believe people would want a computer in their home; DEC (Digital Equipment Corporation) missed the PC market because he ignored customer trends; or Kodak who missed digital photography and kept selling film rolls that you had to process at a favorite drug store.[18] What I have learned from high-tech clients is how heavily matrixed organizations have become. What's worse is that projects are also matrixed, where multiple groups in different countries and reporting structures handle only a subset or only one product feature, making finding a single point of ownership challenging. When geographically dispersed, you are so out of sight and out of mind and everyone is juggling multiple projects, it is virtually impossible to keep everyone updated when things change. The mental model did not evolve to support the implementation, and the result is ineffective decision-making because there are a lot of holes in the information required for a decision.

There was a time in corporate America when good companies were very conscientious. Employees would have a manager whom they could approach to remove obstacles so that the employee would be able to do their job in the best way they could. It's not that these managers no longer exist; their scope of responsibility has changed. They're now doing the work their managers used to do,

---

18   Sutherland, Martin. Organizational Arthritis. 2013.

so they have even more responsibilities now than ever before, which means less control over what they can do to remove those obstacles for their direct reports. First-line managers, in particular, often do two to three jobs – their boss's overflow, their own non-managerial work projects as if they were individual contributors, and their team management job. Guess which one gets sacrificed??

It is no wonder that workplace stress and mental health issues have arisen in the last two decades. Sometimes, what gets in the way of adopting a growth mindset is not always a lack of motivation; it could be the dissatisfaction of knowing that adopting a growth mindset will not change anything- having witnessed what happens when new things are attempted within an arthritic organizational culture.

The average person is often overwhelmed by a flood of opinion-based social media promoting the latest about how they should be thinking and how they should be developing. They don't realize that they may be following the wrong influencer's advice. The apparent need to self-analyze and introspect on every thought and experience has become compulsive in our society. There appears to be a desperate need to find some answer to some question they think is missing. People have become so focused on their own growth that they allow their blind spots and biases to guide them. In the process, they stopped helping others achieve their own growth without understanding the exponential growth that comes from uplifting and assisting others.

An endless need to adopt a growth mindset implies that they are just not good enough as they are. People and organizations prefer to tick boxes without complete and correct implementation that integrates across practices and processes. Without intention, growth mindset becomes harmful and dismissive because people unconsciously fall in love with their own limiting mental models. It is misguided and narrow-minded to believe that others who don't believe what you do are inferior to you in some way. That mental model is judgemental. True growth mindset applies the same reflection to all people equally and with an open mind, suspending our own beliefs and being willing to see things from a radically different perspective.

Why we don't do better: Companies are either busy getting better or busy dying. Consider today's workplace in fast-growing companies or those trying to survive. A happy, steady-state pace no longer exists. Leaders are faced with disruptive innovations and often unexpectedly shifting markets at an unprecedented pace, creating constant stress and chaos.

You're likely thinking, tell me something I don't already know. Okay, here it goes: When the brain is dealing with too much uncertainty - more unknowns than knowns - it cannot do its #1 job of predicting, which frustrates it.

More specifically, it will put you into the Lifecycle of Fear I mentioned in Chapter 2. This is stress. It clouds your vision and cognitive health. In this state, the brain automatically tries to conserve energy and cognitive resources to keep you alive. With the brain focused on conserving energy, it opts for the path of least resistance in other areas. This means you fall back on old bad habits, which are the most established and require the least effort.

Researchers have observed anxiety-related behavior in animals. When our 11-year-old yellow Labrador retriever, Goldie, started to lick an area so much that she created a bald spot, we thought it might be insect-related, but it was not. As she started on other areas, they turned into lesions. The veterinarian confirmed it was skin cancer. Interventions didn't work, and we lost her three months later. In humans, observable behaviors of stressed-out people could be chewing their nails, picking at something, scratching, or other body-focused repetitive behaviors (BFRBs). Dutch researchers published their 2019 study of the brain's response to stress in the journal Brain and Cognition. They found that as the hormone cortisol increased after a threat or challenge, the activity in the goal-directed brain systems tended to diminish, and the established (old) habit-related systems surged.[19]

Tom Smeets, Ph.D., co-author of the study and professor of social and behavioral sciences at Tilburg University

19   https://www.sciencedirect.com/science/article/pii/
       S0278262618300460#b0230

in the Netherlands, concluded that habits demand less cognitive effort and become the default behavior when stressed. A previous study in 2013 published in the Journal of Personality and Social Psychology had reached similar conclusions.[20]

Habit memory is as rigid and inflexible as an organization operating with the 'old guard' top-down, tall-structure approach. They have not learned to adapt to the changing times. This becomes detrimental when circumstances – market shifts, technology disruptions, pandemics - demand a change in behavior, and organizations are not future-ready, agile, and adaptable. I see this all the time. Someone who has worked with one company for many years doing the same type of work will find it incredibly challenging when a new boss implements a different process. Or when someone gets laid off and moves to a different company that has different processes. The 'new' aspects become stressful, so the brain defaults to old habit behaviors and resists the new, which causes more stress. It's a vicious cycle that can cause PTSD and burnout and is not sustainable if not constructively addressed.

That is why establishing good habits is well worth the investment. The operative word is **establishing,** which means it takes time and practice. Leaders unwilling to invest in themselves fall short on growth mindset,

---

20   https://dornsifecms.usc.edu/assets/sites/545/docs/Wendy_ Wood_Research_Articles/Neal_Wood_and_Drolet_2013_JPSP. pdf

emotional intelligence, and adaptability. Worse, they perpetuate these bad habits onto their teams and lose billions of dollars on lost productivity and health costs that hit the bottom line. The point is that companies embracing a learning culture outperform the competition because they are more agile, innovative, and efficient and produce higher-quality products.

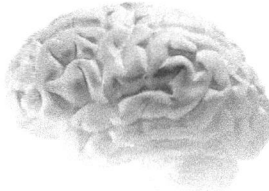

CHAPTER 4

WHY SOCIAL PAIN
IS REAL PAIN

In Chapter 3, I discussed the role that mental models play. How they are born out of subjectively assigning meaning to things or events, and the reason it often inhibits objectivity in our ability to assess situations. When it comes to pain that we feel in our body, most people hold a mental mode that defines pain as being related to tissue damage because of lived experiences that created patterns. For example, you stub your toe or miss your aim with the hammer and get your thumb instead. Ouch! These patterns sound an alarm to the brain to take action to relieve the pain.

Understandably, you apply this rule to all physical pain. It may not occur to you to question whether it could be anything other than a physiological issue because of the existing brain patterns related to pain. You may go to a doctor to figure out the problem, but the doctor will likely interpret the symptoms as a possible illness that matches the symptoms when they don't detect tissue damage. Perhaps it didn't help, or it helped a little bit but not much. Why is that?

To understand the difference between physical and social pain, we must first understand that not all pain is physical damage. Take a sunburn, for example. We don't feel the injury at first until the skin cells begin to die from the damage. This is known as cell apoptosis – a cell's preprogrammed death when the cell is damaged and no longer helpful. Radiation poisoning is another example of delayed cell death after damage from exposure. The reason is that our sensory nervous system does not detect it during the process like smashing your finger with a hammer does.

What's more interesting is that in the case of social pain, alarms sound off in the same manner as physical pain, yet there is no actual physical damage or threat. The pain symptoms may feel the same but are rooted in social pain experiences. Misdiagnosis is only the start of the danger of misunderstanding how the brain works.

Before jumping to the neuroscience of pain and the evidence supporting social pain being the same as physical pain, let's understand the impact of social factors that lead to social pain.

There is a lot of suffering in the world and a million different ways it is expressed because we are all unique. It is not sustainable for humanity to continue operating with blindfolds about 'how' and 'why' pain exists beyond our physical bodies. Alleviating this pain is part of my mission to improve the human condition using ground-breaking brain science and innovation-driven systems and services that enable businesses, individuals, and teams to thrive in an increasingly complex world.

The social pain associated with my behavioral research began with the impact of business disruptions on leaders and their organizations. It was evident during every major technology, industry, market, economic, and political shift over the last several decades. It was also evident during the early stages of the Coronavirus pandemic which led to what I defined as Coronavirus PTSD.

The year 2020 will go down in history as the year of the perfect storm. It was a trifecta that included a deadly pandemic, an unprecedented combination of racial and political unrest in the U.S., and the highest level of economic and health uncertainty the collective world has experienced in centuries.

People were trying to cope with the fallout of the pandemic – whether it was isolation, health issues, grief, anxiety, and unemployment. Facing ongoing uncertainty – not knowing what the future holds – is particularly challenging for the predicting brain because it cannot do its job. For example, the Federal Disaster Distress Mental-health Crisis hotlines saw an 891% spike in calls as reported by

CNN.[21] In short, this depicts the disruptions that I talked about earlier and what led to the Coronavirus PTSD. People suffered simultaneously from physical and social pain, affecting their cognitive functioning and decision-making abilities.

How does this suffering impact the soul?

"My soul is not contained within the limits of my body. My body is contained within the limitlessness of my soul." – Jim Carrey

I'm sitting at the Hard Rock Hotel restaurant in Washington, DC, waiting to place my order. The place is busy, and service is slow. As usual, I scan the room to observe what is going on. I overhear one server griping about something to another server passing by at the dining register. The specifics are unclear, but the tone and emotion are clear. Shortly after, the manager, a thin woman wearing a light gray suit, stops by my table. She asks me if I've been helped. She probably noticed me looking around. I say not yet, and she promptly says she'll get someone to take my order. She closes with 'Have a wonderful day.' A server comes by quickly after that. Before the meal arrives, a commotion arises from the kitchen area, followed by shouts and a scream. A fight has broken out. Soon after, I see an ambulance and the police arriving. They handle

---

21   https://www.cnn.com/2020/04/10/us/disaster-hotline-call-increase-wellness-trnd/index.html

it swiftly through the back door, and customers are not directly disrupted. The rest of the staff carries on business as usual.

When my food arrives, I empathetically comment on how challenging it must be to experience that scene. The server half-jokingly says, *"Well, it's not the first time, so I'm getting used to it."*

I could sense it was an attempt to rationalize the situation to deal with the state of the workplace. He was trying to adjust to a minefield, hoping not to step on one. All the while, I am also observing the actions of the manager. She remains professional and poised. I don't know many people who can maintain composure during this type of disruption, knowing there will be immediate and future ramifications.

I'm thinking, *WOW! This woman is my hero! How does she do it?* As a leadership coach, I had to know. I approach her to give her major kudos and perhaps glean some sage advice from an outstanding leader.

She politely appreciated my compliment after I tell her what I had noticed and how much I admire her calm composure during the incident.

When I ask her, *"How do you do it?"*

She stoically answers, *"Every day after work, I go home and cry."*

The question of whether the soul can hurt has been asked in many different ways. A multitude of articles has been written on this topic alone. This tells me that people sense that something is going on that they feel in their bodies but cannot pinpoint the why or how. From extensive research, observations, working with clients, and personal experience, I can confirm that soul pain is real. As I mentioned earlier, think of it as an accumulation of unpleasant, painful emotions and distress triggered by life's disruptions. Or it could be emotional events like losing a loved one, constant mistreatment by others such as criticizing or bullying, or its ugly cousin, cyberbullying, on social media. It could be humiliation or unresolved problems of shame and guilt that surface with other trauma or events.

As an ardent observer and consulting brain science coach, I'm trained to spot behavioral patterns and identify underlying symptoms that factor into the intersection of cognitive neuroscience and behavioral psychology with human nature, including the soul and a person's perception of it. This is important because the soul is just as vulnerable as the body when subjected to poor habits. It may go largely unnoticed, but the damage is insidious.

Here are some of those soul-damaging habits to avoid:

- **Hanging on to life's poisons**. This includes emotions of hate, grudges, contempt, betrayal, bitterness, and other harm you've felt. This habit is like carrying a bomb that will eventually explode. The burden of these emotions weighs on you and does nothing to those who harmed you.

Do this instead – While anger and hatred are natural responses, the only way to avoid damaging your soul is to let it go. And yes, this means practicing forgiveness. Not for their sake, but for yours. Consider the four levels of forgiveness in Jay Shetty's book 'Think Like a Monk' and make a conscious decision that you can live with without regret:

1. Zero Forgiveness: "I won't forgive you, no matter what."
2. Conditional Forgiveness: "I'll forgive him only if he apologizes."
3. Transformational Forgiveness: In this type of forgiveness, we try to find the strength to forgive a person without needing an apology or expecting anything else in return.
4. Unconditional Forgiveness: This is the kind of forgiveness most parents have for their children. No matter what children do, parents forgive them.

- **Involvement in other people's misery.** We should all know right from wrong, but it is not always easy to know, especially when you are not thinking clearly or considering others. To further complicate things, your complicity could be over a spectrum where one end is apparent, and the other is obscure. Take stealing from someone, for example. It is evident that theft is wrong; however, what if it is driven by an ethical or moral dilemma like stealing food to feed your family? Then there are lesser direct wrongs, like owning a tobacco company or a McDonald's. True, you do not force people to smoke or eat unhealthy food, yet they contribute to the eventual misery of others. You'll discover that the differences between right and wrong become blurred along the spectrum. The point here is not to impose upon you what's right and what's wrong but to encourage you to think and define what's right and wrong for you. Only then can you enhance your soul instead of chipping away at it.

- **Weighing down your soul.** This refers to obsessing over material possessions and riches that essentially shackle your soul, preventing it from flying. Obsession often calls for sacrificing happiness to acquire more material possessions. Other sacrifices include peace and time with loved ones to make more money and buy more stuff. It is likely unnecessary unless it lifts your soul and achieves peace of mind and love. The less attached you are to material possessions, the lighter and freer you will feel.

- **Creating your own limitations.** When you aim too low in what you can achieve, you undermine your soul because the soul is limitless. Nobody craves being mediocre. Instead, people dream of doing extraordinary things but actively limit their aspirations because they fear failing. The paradox is that they are so scared of the pain of failing yet induce soul pain in themselves by not allowing themselves to try. The fear of having bigger goals is temporary once you try and learn and try again. The damage done to the soul can become permanent and continue to erode the soul through regret and blame.

-   **Allowing your ego to dominate**. Your ego is not your amigo. It never has been and never will. The ego seeks to serve itself. The soul seeks to serve others. The ego feels lack, while the soul feels abundance. The ego enjoys the prize. The soul enjoys the journey. The ego is the cause of pain The soul is the cause of healing. The road to happiness and fulfillment is through the soul.

Similar to the ways we can accurately detect the symptoms of PTSD, we can learn to catch the signs of narcissism, authenticity and the strength of the soul. Much of this is intuitive if you pay close attention. For example, have you ever described a piece of music or art as soulful? This is your intuition picking up on signals. Likewise, there are specific signals that may be indicators of people often described as soulless, including:

-   A lack of empathy

- Emotions that seem fake
- Animals don't like them
- They pretend to care
- They lack compassion
- They dislike children, music, and art. They don't 'get it'
- They appear to mimic their surroundings to fit in but lack genuine personal connection

It is important, however, not to apply this indiscriminately because the brain and body are complex, and there is much we do not know. It is wise not to judge because you don't know what they are going through. A trained brain attuned to these signals can also detect when a soul is crying for help because it is hurting, even if the individual does not declare it or is not aware of it. They may even deny it because of their misguided beliefs or biases. Some of the signs are similar to depression, such as:

- Apathy concerning relationships
- Being triggered more easily toward destructive behavior
- Frustration/intolerance
- Fear developed from the seedling of indecision fueled by anxiety and continually fed by uncertainty
- Throwing in the towel; they stop fighting the good fight and give up their agency, feeling helpless
- Asking, 'Why is this happening to me?', unable to achieve clarity and understand themselves

Shaman societies identify loss of soul as a point where a person has stopped dancing, singing, being enchanted by stories, or finding comfort in silence. No matter what your situation is, nobody deserves to suffer. I know because I've been there, and much of this book's inspiration comes from lessons I have taken from my own experiences.

My personal struggle

If I were a betting person, I'd bet this would never happen to me. After all, given my upbringing and zero privilege, I had conquered and defied the odds many times over, but it happened. I fell into clinical depression and suffered from it for two years. Previously a confident over-achiever, creative problem-solver, and conqueror, it would seem unlikely this would happen to me. A car accident in 2014 effectively knocked me off my rails. Initially, the damage was physical, but it seeped into my emotional and psychological state months later. The more I fought and denied it, the deeper I went into the rabbit hole. I was drowning and could see the water's surface above me, but I could not come up for air. I lost relationships and almost lost connection with my family. I also lost the business I had founded ten years earlier. My health was also suffering. I had never had high blood pressure before, but I had progressed to stage two hypertension and was a heart attack waiting to happen. When I finally gave in to seeing a therapist, I refused the idea of taking medication and only agreed to a mild mood enhancer after seven months.

"The soul becomes dyed with the color of its thoughts." – Marcus Aurelius

The back injury was unpleasant and limiting. A neurosurgeon diagnosed me as permanently partially disabled and told me I could never return to the sports I loved, like running and Krav Maga. I was surprised by how much worse the social pain was as the feelings of anger, defeat, shame, anxiety, and fear compounded. I was used to spotting trends and patterns. As if having an out-of-body experience, I could see someone who looked like me but was unrecognizable in every other way. I was aware this was happening but couldn't do anything about it. My soul was hurting.

Desperate to stop the pain, I began researching and learning about cognitive science and behavioral psychology. I wanted to learn how to make my brain work for me and not against me. It took me a whole year just to come clean with my kids about what I was going through and that I was working on a way back. After another year of focused effort, I began to turn the corner.

I take many lessons from this experience. First, disruptions, depression, and other social pain, can happen even to the strongest among us. Second, it is virtually impossible to detect the biases or blind spots that lead you to denial. Third, the pain will compound and dredge previously hidden traumas you had effectively buried but not resolved. Some can even go as far back as childhood traumas. But here's the biggest lesson and one that I promote in my profession:

"You don't ask for help because you are weak. You ask for help because you want to remain strong." – Les Brown

While my experience was painful, it ultimately made me a better human being. I rediscovered myself in all my glory, defects, biases, and blind spots. I now understand how the brain works and how to make it work for me, not against me. I learned why I do what I do. This alone is incredibly empowering and freeing as it breaks the shackles that held me prisoner to my past experiences. I learned what I truly value the most and how to achieve alignment with my intentions and goals. I can confidently say that my life and relationships are better than ever!

Now, I'm more empowered than ever and equipped with tools and techniques to help others become a trifecta: empowered, supernaturally resilient, and future ready. That is why I hope this book reaches as many people as possible, no matter where they are on their journey. Take it from me, don't wait until you become depressed. Don't wait until your body shuts down. Spare yourself of the horrible pain and damage to your soul.

Disruptions are as sure as death and taxes, and they are coming at us faster than ever, as you'll learn in Chapter 6. Becoming resilient and mentally agile is the only way to survive and thrive in a VUCA world. Understanding how you do what you do and why you do what you do is the best gift you can give yourself. You are worth it. Your soul is worth it; you deserve to live the best life possible.

Your soul wants to express itself. Let it.

The neuroscience of social pain and physical pain

People typically believe that social pain comes from stress when you consider that stress is a mental or emotional reaction to adverse or demanding circumstances called stressors. These stressors come from social factors, so it might be easy to deduce that stress causes social pain. But the opposite is true because social pain is one of many social stressors that leads to stress.

Studies conducted by social, clinical, health, and developmental psychologists have explored many aspects of social pain and have shown that social pain is, in fact, the same as physical pain. For example, Dr. Naomi I Eisenberger, Professor and researcher in Social Psychology at UCLS's Department of Psychology provides an accumulation of evidence showing that social pain – the painful feelings following social rejection, exclusion, or loss—relies on some of the same neural circuitry that is involved in processing physical pain.

In 2013, Dr. Eisenberger published her research findings in the Oxford Handbooks Online scholarly research review titled: *"Why Rejection Hurts: The Neuroscience of Social Pain."*[22]

Her research aimed to understand whether an experience of social rejection described as "painful" was primarily metaphorical or whether there is literal truth to that experience. Dr. Eisenberger defines rejection in the context of social pain as referring to being excluded from a social group, whether it be in the workplace, network, neighborhood, or family, to name a few.

When I present on stage on topics like managing disruptions and social stressors, I share her study's image of two different fMRIs (functional MRI – magnetic resonance imaging). One image is based on research studying physical pain, showing the brain area that activates when physical pain is experienced. The other image studying social pain also marks the area that is activated. When the images were compared side by side, there is a distinct overlap between the brain's circuitry that processes social pain and physical pain as seen here

---

22 https://www.oxfordhandbooks.com/view/10.1093/oxford-hb/978019539870C.001.0001/oxfordhb-9780195398700-e-15#ox-fordhb-9780195398700-div2-113

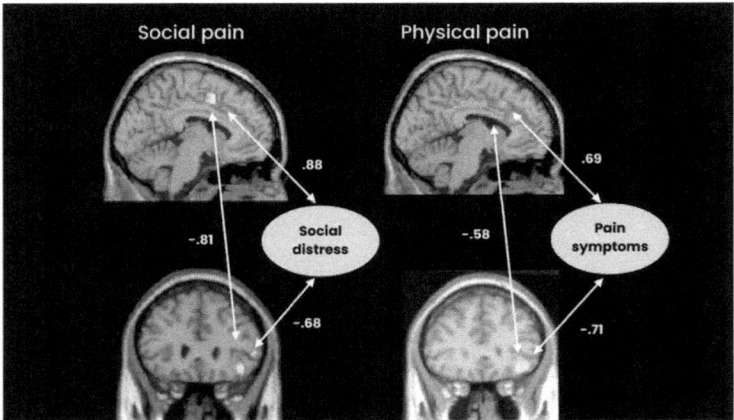

Building on this overlap in the neural circuitry that underlies physical and social pain, it is also essential to consider several consequences of this shared circuitry. Additional experiments also revealed that:

- Individuals who are more sensitive to one kind of pain are also more sensitive to the other.

- Factors that typically alter one type of pain (e.g., Tylenol reduces physical pain) can alter the other (e.g., Tylenol also reduces social pain).

Given my expertise in technology and innovation convergence, it was fascinating to hear the story of how this discovery came about. In an interview by Yale University's Experts in Emotion Series, Dr. Eisenberger recounts what led to her focus on the correlation between social and physical pain.

She had been putting together experiments to determine how the brain processes rejection. Using fMRI scanners, they brought people in to participate in a game of Cyberball, an online game where the computer controls two players, but the person believes they are playing with two other real people. The ball is tossed around to all the players. After a while, the non-human computer players stop throwing the ball to the human. The subject is essentially socially excluded, allowing Dr. Eisenberg to capture brain scans of what the brain was doing during that time.

When she got the data back and analyzed it, she was sitting next to a fellow graduate student analyzing a study on physical pain from patients experiencing chronic pain such as IBS (irritable bowel syndrome). With their data up on the computer screens, at some point, they noticed how similar the data looked from two very different studies. Based on that, looking further into the connection between those two made sense.

Similar studies are explained in the book "*Social Pain: Neuropsychological and Health Implications of Loss and Exclusion*" by Geoff MacDonald and Lauri A. Jensen-Campbell, and these offer a comprehensive, multidisciplinary exploration of social pain- the experience of pain as a result of interpersonal rejection or loss.

The research on this phenomenon continues to get more attention as discoveries emerge. In many ways, our future continues to depend on it. Why? Because we have equal capacity to destroy or to save ourselves. The problem is that in an increasingly complex world, we do not notice or listen to the signs that tell us which way we are going until the damage is done. This is the reason there is a mental health crisis.

The mind-body connection and impact

The need for human connection goes back to the survival of mammalian species in general, and it is why we are social animals. The theory is that it is likely that through evolution, the social sensors piggybacked on the pain sensors to alert us when our bodies were in danger, both physical and social. For the development of the human race, it is no different. We are hard-wired with the need to belong because our very lives depend on being part of a tribe. Our earliest ancestors learned there was no chance of survival and passing on their genes without belonging.

The theory is supported by studies done with infants who received no human connection compared to those that did. John Bowlby is recognized as the originator of the attachment theory. A British psychologist and psychoanalyst, Bowlby believed early childhood attachments played a critical role in later development and mental functioning. The attachment theory focuses on relationships and bonds with those who can provide nurturance, comfort, and safety that ensure the child's survival. For example, when children are frightened, they seek their primary caregiver to give them comfort and care, creating behavioral and motivational patterns.[23]

In Chapter 2, I described the neuroscience of fear and how it is a construct of our minds. The possibility of rejection threatens our need to belong. This is why rejection is the kind of experience that can change your emotions significantly, and the effects can be immediate through sounding alarms.

If, for example, you are giving a speech and start to feel like you are being evaluated and might be rejected, your organ and body sensors pick up on this thought (perceived danger or threat). This part of the process is driven by emotions interpreted into thoughts in your mind. Those thoughts drive your organs to react, your heart starts pumping faster, and your mouth gets dry. These physical reactions sound the alarms and notify the brain, which compares the alarms to patterns previously established and predicts what the body needs to survive – the brain's number one priority. It starts to pump the specific types of chemicals to your body to address its needs (recall the body budgeting of resources in Chapter 1.)

It is essential to know that there are many forms of perceived or actual rejection from different social factors. Here are some examples:

---

23   https://www.verywellmind.com/john-bowlby-biogra-phy-1907-1990-2795514

1. The psychological effects on adopted adults: Studies have shown that adopted adults suffer from underlying problems such as the ability to develop an identity, reduced self-esteem and self-confidence, higher risk of mental health disorders, and more are reported by the Center for Treatment of Anxiety and Mood Disorders. In a study by Silverstein and Kaplan, seven core issues were identified that still hold true today. They are Loss, Rejection, Guilt/Shame, Grief, Identity, Intimacy, and Mastery/Control. These are all painful emotions that I explore later in this chapter.

    With the advent of technological innovations from DNA testing companies that make it possible to locate biologically connected families, this issue has grown and become front and center for adoptees. I've observed similar patterns, having sensed a looming cloud on every person I've spoken to who discovered relatives they never knew existed. Outwardly, they express curiosity, interest, and excitement about meeting these newfound family members. Yet when I gently probe, the stress of whether this family will accept or [also] reject them is revealed. Even before technology, an adopted child often feels a level of rejection by the biological parents regardless of having loving adoptive parents. They can carry a sense of social rejection with them throughout their lives.[24]

2. Parental abandonment is another form of rejection. It happens when a parent walks away from the family, accepting no responsibility for their well-being, or when the parents go through a divorce. In either case, it can be psychologically devastating to a child who does not possess the ability to comprehend the situation, even if the separation was necessary to ensure the safety and protection of the child.

3. In the workplace, rejection takes many forms. It could be driven by unconscious biases based on race, ethnicity, age, gender expression, sexuality, or unexamined assumptions (more on this later). Increased awareness and social pressure have moved companies towards adopting some level of diversity and inclusion programs. It's a start, but it depends on the program's execution, implementation, and adherence. When evaluating a company's programs related to employee engagement, performance, or retention, I can assess whether they are authentic, implemented correctly, and will achieve the intended behavioral changes.

24 https://www.centerforanxietydisorders.com/what-prob-lems-do-adopted-adults-have/#:~:text=Rejection%20is%20part%20of%20the,the%20adoptee's%20feelings%20of%20rejec-tion

4. Other forms of rejection include feeling excluded from social gatherings like work lunches, inattentive audience when presenting, losing a client, losing a relationship, or consistently being picked last for a team.

Because this feels so uncomfortable and threatening, given our ancestrally programmed need to belong to survive, people go to great lengths to avoid rejection. Outside of business, it means trying to fit in. In industry, it is called herd mentality or groupthink. In either case, you follow everyone else at your expense. You develop a pattern of fear and avoidance of certain activities that can potentially induce that horrible feeling. But this is not the answer, as it will bind you to that fear the longer you hold on to it. In my article, *"Beyond Emotional Intelligence – Workplace Conflict, Avoidance Coping, and the Mental Health Crisis"*, I describe a maladaptive mechanism called avoidance coping. This form of coping intervenes to keep a person from facing the possibility that experiencing rejection is a form of personal failure. It is, therefore, critical to address it. The answer is to be acutely aware and develop the courage to face it. Only then can it be conquered and managed.[25]

Beware what you fight for because
you may just get to keep it.

---

25 https://adrianavela.expert/beyond-emotional-intelligence-work-place-conflict-avoidance-coping-and-the-mental-health-crisis/

How is pain created?

Let's dig deeper to understand how pain is created and its associated emotions. In a recent article from Science Focus, authors of the book *"Ouch! – Why Pain Hurts, and Why It Doesn't Have To"*, Margee Kerr and Linda Rodriguez McRobbie talk about how the brain creates pain.[26]

They also shed light on Dr. Lisa Feldman Barrett's book, *"How Emotions Are Made"* and how, as a lived experience, we understand pain as an alarm system that alerts us to tissue damage that has occurred or the threat that it is about to. Interestingly, the patterns we have created based on lived experience bias the perception of our body's response to the threat of pain. These patterns provide contextual information above and beyond the sensory input. Contextual information includes the situational needs and motivations at the time, who is present, whether we have any control over the situation, and our expectations.

CONTEXTUAL INFORMATION

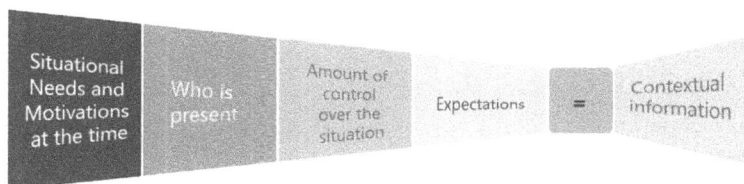

Situational Needs and Motivations at the time | Who is present | Amount of control over the situation | Expectations | = | Contextual information

---

26 https://www.sciencefocus.com/the-human-body/how-your-brain-creates-pain-and-what-we-can-do-about-it/

One example is when a child gets a vaccine for the first time, and they have an older sibling who describes the worst possible pain. Another example is someone defocusing from their painful fingers after the door closes on them because they're entering the interview for the job of their dreams.

In these cases, the child may or may not have experienced a jab before, but either the fear emotion brought on by the sibling's emotions or the previous unpleasant experience provides the brain with strong information to predict what is about to happen. In the interview case, the brain is so preoccupied with the intense focus on the importance of the interview, based on previous patterns (lived experiences), that it will provide the body with the resources to complete the task. The resource is a release of internal natural opioids called endorphins as pain relief for the jammed fingers in this case. The interview has taken priority over the pain.

Why is this? Sensory organs – eyes, ears, nose, mouth, temperature, central nervous system, etc. – flood the brain with ambiguous information. Creating simulations is the brain's way of guessing what is happening in the world and making sense of it. As more patterns develop over time, the brain creates concepts that are used as cookie cutters to make sense of future sensory input.

Another fascinating discovery in the British Medical Journal reported that neuroscientists can observe the pain signature in the brain as reported by patients who had no tissue damage at all. This means that pain does not require tissue damage to be felt—for example, phantom limb pain in amputees or the pain of depression or grief.

"*Consider the story of the construction worker who stepped on a 15-centimeter-long nail. The nail punctured his boot, and even the smallest movement was agony. After sedation with some pretty serious narcotics, the team at the hospital was able to extract the nail, and low and behold, 'When they removed his boot, a miraculous cure seemed to have taken place,' the British Medical Journal reported the nail had slid between his toes and the foot was entirely uninjured (no word on his pride, however).*"[11]

The complex nervous system network manages nonstop processing and integrating of information, internal regulation, calibration, and balancing as it communicates with the brain so that the brain can do its predictive work as the central command center for your body.

With the goal of predictive and efficient regulation of physiological processes necessary for our survival, the brain learns how to adapt to the environment and predict what the body will need to prepare to meet those needs.

Dr. Lisa Feldman Barrett describes the neuronal firing based on best guesses of what is about to happen next. She says that we construct and run our own internal model, or simulation, of our lived reality almost as if a bridge is forming just as you put your foot down on it, microseconds ahead of your conscious awareness.

Have you ever experienced the surprise (and jolt) when you realize the curb you stepped off was higher than anticipated? That's an example of where the brain gets it wrong. This means that the signals received from our simulations are felt just as intensely as the signals we get from the nerve cells when tissue damage occurs. Case in point is the unfortunate builder who stepped on the nail was really a victim of his own predictive processing, and his internal simulation of that injury sounded the alarm.

Another way of understanding this concept from the brain's perspective is to imagine the brain as the pilot of a sophisticated aircraft. It depends only on the technology sensors and instrumentation to successfully carry out the job of reaching a destination. The pilot (brain) cannot do this without the information from the instruments, but it does know the protocols (patterns) from training and experience and also uses that knowledge to take appropriate action.

To say that's all the brain does is a massive oversimplification. That's like saying that nanotechnology is small yet having no idea just how small 10^{-9} is unless you get some perspective. One nanometer in length is roughly the size of 6-8 atoms in a row or one billionth of a meter. Now, think of the brain as not just piloting one aircraft, but managing the entire global air transportation system, the communication, the routing, and scheduling – not just the plane en route, but every activity that goes on at each terminal across the globe every second of every day.

Be kind to your brain – it is impressively powerful but also delicate!

Key Takeaway: The most important and empowering point is knowing that pain is a complex and multi-layered experience driven less by proximate cause and more by what we think, fear, and our expectations of pain at a conscious and non-conscious level.

Exploring Other Painful Emotions – Anger, Guilt, Shame, Resentment, and Grief

"An emotion is your brain's creation of what your bodily sensations mean in relation to what is going on around you in the world." Lisa Feldman Barret.

Since I already discussed the emotion of rejection as part of the research on social and physical pain, I'll now touch on other painful emotions often linked to destructive behaviors and negative physiological issues. My primary goal is to let you know that I observe, listen, and feel your pain. I am dedicated to improving your human condition for your benefit, for the benefit of society, and for our future.

Anger: Would it surprise you that someone who may appear calm and collected could really be pissed off? How about a person who is unaware of how angry they are? Depending on the individual, they could be a heart attack waiting to happen, unexpectedly go postal one day, or decide to commit suicide – the adage 'depression is anger turned on itself' holds true. You see, not everyone who is angry shows it. In fact, not everyone is fully aware of it because it could be buried in the unconscious until it is triggered. It could be that they learned to force themselves to avoid expressing emotions or were taught to ignore it and toughen up to be a good leader. Or else, they hide it because they learned that anger is not a socially acceptable emotion. Perhaps they're simply not self-aware enough to realize a potential silent self-sabotage pattern is brooding inside them because they tell themselves lies or have misguided beliefs that cause them to suppress or ignore this emotion. In any case, unexamined anger silently chips away at their soul and blocks them from having the life they deserve. When we add a personal and social component to anger, it turns into outrage carrying with it a response of betrayal or personal transgression.

"Beware the unloved for someday they could hurt themselves, or me." – Jim Carrey

Contemporary to the late 2010s and early 2020s, most expressions of outrage and anger took the form of what's called 'the cancel culture.' Cancel culture, or call-out culture, refers to a form of ostracism in which someone is thrust out of social or professional circles – whether online, on social media, or in person. Those subject to this ostracism are said to have been "canceled." Of course, ongoing controversies and debates exist on whether this culture ultimately results in increased accountability or censorship. Whatever your beliefs, a lot of finger-pointing and blaming triggers a sense of betrayal or transgression, often expressed as outrage. You see this all the time on social media, ranging from speaking up to bullying disguised as First Amendment rights.

The Positive Side of Anger

Anger is a principal emotion in the same way that joy and happiness are. We are evolutionarily wired for anger to help ensure our survival. For example, moral outrage will mobilize action and expose wrongdoers and injustices in the world. It motivates the fight against the oppression of human rights, abuse, and other atrocities that threaten our survivability. Accessing and focusing on anger can relieve anxiety and depression and boost your energy, clarity, and productivity. Anger with a clear purpose to right a wrong is necessary. Think of taxation without representation that led to the Declaration of Independence that created the United States. Likewise, the women's suffrage movement from 1848-1917 achieved women's right to vote.

The problem with anger starts when it is suppressed and unmanaged because it loses its purpose.

Problem: It does not matter how good you have become at hiding your anger, it will come out one way or another. Sweeping it under the rug does not mean it's not there. The anger emotion never goes away until the brain has processed it to make sense of it. If not fully processed, it remains an unresolved issue that the brain does not forget. The brain is amazing because it can do this and simultaneously address sensory alarms and body budgeting to keep the cells in your body alive. During these times, a person would feel stuck or trapped, thus triggering other emotions to join in on the misery train – rage, shame, guilt, helplessness, or others, all of which are hard to work through. You feel vulnerable and emotionally exhausted, robbing you of the energy you need to enjoy your life with your loved ones and achieve your goals. Furthermore, whether expressed or not, your anger could lead to what we know as "Emotional Hijacking." It happens to even the most level-headed people. When triggered, they seem to morph into a completely different person - almost like a Jekyll and Hyde persona.

Emotional hijacking is similar to being pushed out of the driver's seat and taken somewhere you do not want to go. Interestingly, emotional hijacking is often rooted in the perceived fear of not being allowed control of a situation or our ability to change it. Fear is a powerful emotion that paralyzes and blocks your pre-frontal cortex from taking rational action. Because fear is a heightened response in the body, the brain releases cortisol to keep it alert and adrenaline to prepare it for a fight or flight response, even if you don't have a lion chasing you. This is why you end up feeling stressed and anxious and unable to think straight when emotionally hijacked. Think of it as seeing 'red', limiting your ability to see a clear path to navigate the situation in this state. You end up with a flood of emotions, such as regret, shame, or guilt accompanied by added anxiety, stress, worry, or fear of the consequences. It's not a pretty picture, I know. Learning to regulate your emotions is one part of developing emotional intelligence.

What can you do?

First, practice self-compassion and remind yourself that we are all human. Beating yourself up is counterproductive. Second, life does suck sometimes, and you are not the only one who has lost their cool. Start by recognizing that anger is a basic human emotion. Like other basic emotions, you cannot eliminate them. Emotions are tied to our ability to survive and have been honed throughout history. Anger can prepare you to fight and defend yourself against a threat. Not all anger is destructive. I mentioned earlier how benevolent anger can mobilize you to combat injustices. Emotional hijacking, however, has a transformational effect resembling the Tasmanian Devil in the Warner Bros. Looney Tunes cartoons. If you are wondering why there is a drastic turn in metaphors, it's because reading about emotions tends to illicit your own emotions by drawing on past experiences, so take a mental breath and laugh a little. I am.

Anger is always associated with a trigger event that is currently happening, which engages the neurosympathetic nervous system. It could also be an unresolved past event that resurfaces as a result of a current triggering event, which blends and amplifies the anger. Rumination, the tendency to dwell on past mistakes, losses, failures, or wrongs done to you, could be another trigger that brings about the anger emotion. Some people are misguided in believing that unleashing the anger will be cathartic and that they'll feel better. Sadly, that is never the case. While getting it off your chest may feel justified and good in the moment, it does not last. Instead, you have further burdened yourself with different emotions such as remorse, guilt, and shame. The best path is understanding the anger's root and its triggers. It also helps to consider the consequences of suppressing or not regulating anger. Unchecked, the result is chronic anxiety – prolonged worry and anxiety disorder intense enough that it interferes with daily activities. Unacknowledged anger also leads to other health and psychological issues. It's a high price to pay.

Here are three actionable steps to begin a productive journey toward getting back in the driver's seat so that you don't get taken where you don't want to go.

1. Know yourself first – Understanding what makes you tick and what ticks you off is essential. Not just what, but also why. Working with a trained professional is the most effective way to accomplish this. Options to consider are certified experts in emotional intelligence training, a certified brain science coach, or a psychologist. It is prudent to avoid any of the personality tests you find online that are free or popular without proper qualifying criteria because those will only give you a piece of the puzzle of who you are. Furthermore, insist that behavior or personality tools you consider show proof of validation for accuracy and reliability, that they are 100% bias-free and validated by the neuroscience community. We all need someone else to help us objectively pinpoint where we are and where we need to go. The right person with the appropriate tools and techniques will help you uncover unresolved anger and why you are triggered so you know what to look for and take preventive action. I provide a list of recommended resources at the end of this book to help you on this journey.

2. Self-regulate – There are many approaches and techniques to de-escalating emotions of anger to suit your preferences. We are all unique, and there is no one-size-fits-all approach. Meditation is a prevalent method, but some may see it as esoteric or ethereal, and that's okay. It is not for everyone. But there are other techniques, such as box breathing, which is so effective that the U.S. Navy Seals use it to perform under the most excruciatingly stressful situations [27] It is good to remember that just because you do not outwardly express anger or you

---

27 (https://www.forbes.com/sites/nomanazish/2019/05/30/
    how-to-de-stress-in-5-minutes-or-less-according-to-a-navy-
    seal/?sh=120563d83046)

are not being destructive to others, that it is not there. It simply means that the destruction is unto you.

3. Move – Tony Robbins is known to say, 'Motion creates emotion,' so when it comes to emotional hijacking, you need to move to break the natural fear response tendency of fight, flight, or freeze and lock up. It is most important to break the body's state and shift it by moving, even if it is just going outside or to another room. Change the view so your body's sensors capture new inputs and unlock the body when things get emotionally charged. A new environment means new sensors – visual, audible, and others enter the brain and help create a pathway to assess the situation more rationally. We can't always succeed and eliminate emotional hijacking entirely, but we can certainly begin to ease its negative impact on our relationships, health, and business.

A psychologist at the Cognitive Behavioral Institute of Albuquerque, Nick Wignall, author of *"Find Your Therapy"* suggests looking for signs of:

- Chronic Anxiety
- Rumination
- Passive-Aggressive Communication
- Venting
- Hypercriticism

These signs tend to indicate that a person is angrier than they think.

Key Takeaway: Anger and outrage are not intrinsically bad. They can mobilize action and expose wrongdoers and injustices. Recognizing and acknowledging your anger before responding is crucial to understanding its roots, its triggers, and its consequences.

Guilt and Shame: These two emotions are closely related. According to research from Daniel Sznycer, social psychologist and Assistant Professor at the University of Montreal, they are not emotions to dread because they are the emotions that nudge us to behave better. He says, "When we act in a way we are not proud of that elicits regret, the brain broadcasts a signal that prompts us to alter our conduct." It is part of our ability to adapt to an environment and remain part of a tribe that allows us to survive. It is part of our hard-wired DNA.

Guilt's purpose was to make us kinder and more giving. In short, they are self-conscious emotions linked to real or perceived moral failures, which keep us from destroying ourselves and those around us.

On the other hand, shame is based on the fear of others finding out about your social transgressions, knowing that your moral compass will be damaged as perceived by others. Sometimes shame is born out of crimes done to a person, such as child abuse or rape victims made to feel it was their fault or believe speaking out will make it worse for them.

Shame, in particular, is viewed as the ugly cousin of guilt. Still, it kept us alive by protecting us from harming those dear to us and promoting better behavior as we evolved. If you were not liked in the tribe, it would be a death sentence because people had to rely on each other to survive.

The main difference between the two is that guilt can occur and not involve anyone else because it is based on knowing that you did something you are not proud of, and realizing it, you try to make it up to the person you harmed or remedy the situation somehow. It occurs when your behavior conflicts with your conscience.

Brain activity also differs according to fMRI (functional MRI) studies by German scientists from Ludwig-Maximilian-University in Munich. Guilt states showed neural activity in the amygdala and frontal lobes but less activity in both brain hemispheres. Shame states set off high activity in the right part of the brain but not the amygdala. They concluded shame is a more complex emotion given its broad cultural and social factors, while guilt is linked only to a person's learned social standards.

Problem: Despite the benefit of keeping us on the straight and narrow, shame and guilt are among the most painful of human emotions. Guilt focuses on behavior and tells you, "*I did something bad.*" Shame is focused on the self and tells you, "*I am bad.*" The emotion of shame is so strong that it could lead to more transgressions to cover up the evidence or lying for fear of being exposed. Brené Brown, a five-time New York best-selling author and research professor at the University of Houston and the University of TX Austin McCombs School of Business, studied courage, vulnerability, shame, and empathy for two decades. She firmly believes that you must walk through vulnerability to courage; therefore, Embrace The Suck. Her current motto is 'Courage over comfort.' She says, *"There is also a high correlation between shame and addiction, depression, violence, aggression, bullying, suicide, and eating disorders, while guilt is inversely correlated with those things."*[28]

What can you do? Guilt does not define you as a person, it defines behavior that harmed another person. For that, the antidote is owning the behavior and apologizing by making amends. Shame is a whole other ball of wax; every human experiences shame unless they are a sociopath. From years of study and research, I've learned that human nature will drive us to great lengths and effort to avoid facing shame. Yet, this is precisely where we need to start because it will be your ongoing roadblock to recovery if you want to live a fulfilled life and achieve self-acceptance. The most critical antidote for shame is empathy. Once you have acknowledged the shame by identifying the negative thought patterns, it is important to accept the feeling and know that everyone else goes through it, too – you're not alone. Now consider forgiving

---

28   TEDx https://www.youtube.com/watch?v=psN1DORYYV0

yourself and telling yourself, "I'll do better next time." This is not easy, but it is necessary. Being compassionate and forgiving yourself improves your self-esteem and self-worth because you learn lessons from it and take action to ensure it does not happen again.

> *"I encourage people to remember that 'no' is a complete sentence." – Gavin de Becker*

Resentment – Resentment is an underlying sense of being mistreated. It combines three emotions: painful bitterness + anger + past injuries. It is about how we were 'wronged,' 'made to suffer,' humiliated, or other. Vehemently hanging on to past injuries is what eventually defines you. Worse, resentment becomes the anchor that sinks you to the ocean floor where you can't come up for air. The more you hang on to it, the more you set yourself up for aroused anger or provocation if the person you resent is recognized. It typically manifests when a person habitually complains about that past injury and then complains more when others don't truly understand their suffering. In short, they can't let go. It sounds simple, but it's not.

Problem – Years of study, observation, and addressing my own emotions have taught me it is essential to understand that letting go of resentment is not a decision one makes. It is a habit that needs to be developed and honed. Creating a new habit takes time, deliberate practice, and commitment to building. Tenacity is vital because the existing mental model has been continually reinforced for years or even decades. Simply deciding that you will let go will, therefore, fail. It is not a battle of wills but intention. Deciding to start working on it is an excellent first step. Resentment can grow inside you and fester. Not addressing it will erode your mental clarity and self-esteem, damaging your soul and emotional and physical homeostasis.

What can you do? Start taking action in the same way you would start a goal-oriented training program like weightlifting or running. It would be best if you were patient and keep practicing. Practice telling yourself that it is not about how justified you are to feel resentment. It is about moving from the past to the present moment. Practice reminding yourself that resentment harms you and only prolongs the pain. If you feel pulled to the past injury, practice refocusing your attention. Notice what is going on in front of you. With training and practice, you will build the strength to accept, forgive, and lay that past injury to rest – R.I.P!

Grief – When we think of grief, we think of the pain associated with someone's death. Grief is a natural reaction to loss that can take many forms. This is why many people suffer from grief and don't realize it. For example, in the United States, we grieved as a nation after the terrorist attack at the World Trade Center in NY on 9/11/2001. I learned of the attack during a conference in Los Angeles, CA, where I was enjoying dinner and conversation with one of our clients, the Chief Technology Officer of the Nasdaq Stock Exchange, and his wife. I could sense the fear and concern as they excused themselves to call back home. As a safety precaution and consideration, the remainder of the conference was canceled, and I packed up to drive back to my home in San Jose, CA. During part of my drive home, I called my husband, assuring him I was okay and being vigilant and staying away from high-density locations. Because I've always been a systems thinker (I go into debug mode), my brain was busily trying to make sense of the magnitude of the impact of this event. Although I use the analogy of going into debug mode from my previous life as a programmer, systems thinking is a way of making sense of the world's complexity by applying neuroscience, biology, politics, economics, and more and looking at the interconnectivity of multiple variables at play instead of individually and seeking more information as needed.

At that time, I had not yet mastered the whole of systems thinking but had developed an inclination toward it. Therefore, I searched for patterns to make sense of the psychological impact this would have on the victims of the attack and their families. Not once did it occur to me to pay attention to what was happening inside me. I dismissed the possibility of any direct impact, feeling grateful that I did not have family or business travel there. It wasn't until two or three weeks later, when I was preparing to go to bed, that I began sobbing suddenly and very much unexpectedly. Nothing happened leading up to my sobbing. I was not consciously feeling sad or hurt leading up to it. At first, I did not know why until I was curious enough to dig deeper into my emotions and found the connection to 9/11. With more analysis (here comes my debug mode again), I began to understand that I was grieving the loss of my general sense of safety as a citizen. Something that many of us have taken for granted. We don't have to go back that far to understand global grief as the world has experienced it with the COVID-19 pandemic. Once again, in this example, you'll find a cacophony of emotions that embody non-death-related grief.

Problem: Part of the biggest problem is that the pandemic is not over, and the threat continues. Clinical social workers and mental health hotlines consistently report on the pandemic's grief-related emotional, psychological, and cognitive impact on people, even if no death was involved. Grief comes from losing anyone or anything with deep attachment. It could be the loss of moving around freely and safely, a job you loved, the loss of economic stability, or something else you unexpectedly lost. Unfortunately, humans tend to compare themselves and dismiss the feeling of grief as only being real or valid when it involves someone close to them dying. Therefore, we struggle, and our brains frustrate because the mental models do not fit the sensory input. It cannot make sense of that general feeling of discombobulation.

When this emotion is not honored, it becomes trapped. Eventually, it shows up in other ways, such as physical, emotional, and spiritual exhaustion, threatening your immune system and leading to further health issues. Discombobulated is how the brain feels because it constantly tries to figure out how to survive by predicting in the face of pure uncertainty. Are you properly social distancing? Does that person look sick? Are they showing symptoms? I'm feeling a sore throat- am I getting sick? Will I lose my job? And so on and so on. The brain is pre-wired to predict and do body budgeting, so it frustrates and suffers when it can't do its job.

What can you do? The first step is recognizing that a non-death-related loss also leads to grief and that it is not just okay to feel it but also a natural human behavior to grieve any loss. Second, restoration and gratitude are essential because dealing with loss is exhaustive and drains your energy. Remember, the brain spends extra resources processing emotions and working extra hard trying to predict what comes next to do its body budgeting and provide your body with the resources it needs. The body needs to have the chance to replenish those spent resources. I'm not suggesting you ignore or set aside your sadness to accomplish this. It means being present with your sorrow and holding on to all the things you are grateful for at the same time. Doing so is helpful in your grieving journey as you go through it and allow the brain to process it with the help of restorative efforts such as sleep, exercise, being with loved ones, and humor.

Even crying and screaming can help the healing process. It is about self-care, staying connected with others, and knowing you are valuable and vital, therefore, worth being present for yourself and not just for others. There is no playbook for navigating grief because it is different for everyone. The goal is to set a path toward healing and going from the depths of grief to a place of gratitude.

Key lessons– Emotions are complex and have a natural life cycle – a beginning, a middle, and an end. Nothing lasts forever unless you get trapped in the middle. Even when the problem or initial trigger is gone, the emotion will stay until your brain has fully processed it from beginning to end. Sounds easy, right? Sadly, it is not because self-sabotaging emotions like shame, fear, guilt, or others may push you to avoid the pain and bury the emotion instead of confronting it. Trapped emotions easily lead to emotional exhaustion, usually the first sign of burnout.

Another pattern I see is when some people refer to emotions as either good or bad. There is no such thing as good or bad emotions. Just because an emotion *feels* bad doesn't mean it is *bad* or you *are* bad for feeling it. The key is not to judge our emotions but to understand the event that triggered the feelings for what it is. Life dishes out good and bad experiences; it is human nature to feel emotions toward those events. If we stop labeling them as good or bad, we will make huge strides in preventing trapped emotions that do damage in the background. Instead, you can productively address them by acknowledging, facing, honoring, accepting, and deconstructing them. We resolve them and keep them from holding us hostage, preventing us from moving forward. In Chapter 8, I provide an array of techniques that help you build resilience and achieve self-mastery.

Key Takeaway: The brain is the architect of emotions. Although I touched on specific emotions independently, it is crucial to recognize that many of these emotions travel in groups and are not mutually exclusive. The ingredients that create emotions, Context, Patterns, Body State, and Language are shown in the diagram below. The more we understand them, the more resilient we can be against social pain.

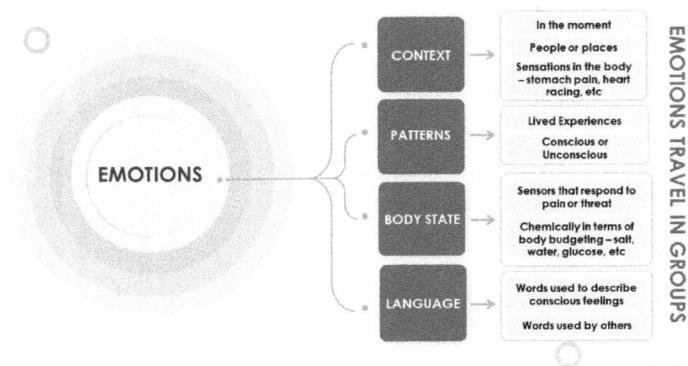

If you or your team suffer from social pain, know you are not alone. Also, know that courage and fortitude are required to take that step towards understanding and addressing the pain head-on. It feels impossible because our instinct is to avoid facing the pain. We want to get away from it.

That's human nature. However, you must be aware that it will also require courage and fortitude to live with the pain of carrying the baggage of unresolved issues for the rest of your life. The cost is the same, but the outcome is very different. Remember, you are a product of your decisions.

Acceptance is a critical first step. Accept that you are in pain, and it sucks. Then, separate yourself from the emotion and see it for what it is: an experience and feeling you have. It is not your identity.

Social pain and all the accompanying emotions that whittle at your soul lose their power when you permit yourself to face them. Nothing changes without this first step.

"The most difficult thing is the decision to act. The rest is merely tenacity." – Amelia Earhart

When I finally permitted myself to accept that I had fallen into clinical depression after my car accident, it marked the time I began the healing process. Until then, I was in denial, rejecting the thought that this was possible. After all, I had conquered so much and was a smart cookie. It was nonsense to think that, because I was biased in my thinking, depression only happened to people who were of weaker character. I'm embarrassed to admit it, but that is the nature of our biases and blind spots, as I later learned. Coming to terms with the impact of being diagnosed as permanently partially disabled and that I would never be able to run races or go back to Krav Maga was a blow that hit me harder than I realized. I grieved for losing the go-getter abilities that had defined me for so long. I grieved from realizing that the Adriana Vela I previously knew was no longer. I hardly recognized the person in the mirror and didn't like what I saw as my health was deteriorating when I couldn't find a way out.

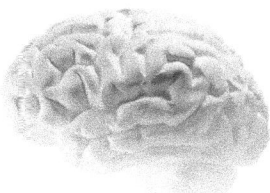

CHAPTER 5

TOXIC POSITIVITY

Toxic positivity is a thing, and perhaps the worst unintended consequence originating from the positive thinking movement. What is toxic positivity?

"Toxic positivity is a way of responding to your own or someone else's suffering that comes across as a lack of empathy. It dismisses emotions instead of affirming them and could come from a place of discomfort." - Tabith Kirkland, psychologist and associate professor at the University of Washington's Department of Psychology.

Toxic positivity results in denial, minimization, and invalidation of the authentic human emotional experience. Well-intentioned expressions like "Well at least..." "It could be worse" or "Look on the bright side" are all examples of toxic positivity. There's nothing wrong with being able to express positive thoughts; however, the point where it rejects where others are coming from or that their situation is a problem they are struggling with is a simplified definition of toxic positivity. Think of it this way. This exchange is no different from a person with a very stern religious belief who refuses to listen to people with contradictory views and forces their beliefs onto them. If positivity was a religion, and a person was deeply faithful to positivity, they would not want to hear anything other than that faith and actively reject hearing anything different. People are often over-invested in the growth mindset as a self-development approach that leads to overdosing on positivity to the extent that it becomes toxic. Fig X lists examples of toxic positivity as distinguished from empathetic responses.

Toxic Positivity
Examples of Toxic & Accepting Statements

Toxic Positivity	Non-Toxic Acceptance & Validation
"Don't think about it, stay positive!"	"Describe what you're feeling, I'm listening."
"Don't worry be happy!"	"I see that you're really stressed, anything I can do?"
"Failure is not an option."	"Failure is a part of growth and success."
"Everything will work out in the end."	"This is really hard, I'm thinking of your."
"Positive vibes only!"	"I'm here for you through both good and bad."
"If I can do it, so can you!"	"Everyone's story, abilities, limitations are different, and that's ok."
"Delete Negativity."	"Suffering is a part of life, you are not alone."
"Look for the silver lining."	"I see you I'm here for you."
"Everything happens for a reason."	"Sometimes we can draw the short straw in life. How can I support you during this hard time?"
"It could be worse."	"That sucks. I'm so sorry you're going through this."

Fig X Toxic and non-toxic response examples.

Toxic positivity does not help you build healthy relationships, including the relationship you have with yourself. There is a negative impact on your relationship with yourself because you lie to yourself and continue to be in denial about your issues or problems. People tend to deny them because facing their issues related to their emotions is so painful that they will do just about anything to avoid it. The denial tendency is a dysfunctional coping behavior and an example of avoidance coping that I discussed in Chapter 4. The collateral damage to the brain's pattern processes and your soul is significant, yet it disguises itself as just being 'positive.' You may be able to fool yourself or others, but you will not be able to fool your soul.

Impact on self

Clinical psychologist Barbara Held supports the concept of toxic positivity and uses it to help those suffering from severe denial of their problems break through the block that prevents them from acknowledging that there is a problem in the first place. Often, people are in denial that they are unhappy. I have experienced people like this. I can tell that they are not happy, that they are struggling with something, but they will not allow themselves to feel it, much less confront it. When that happens, the issues they're battling with will get stronger and more suppressed, and the more suppressed they are, the more they cut across other parts of their lives - not just the area where the issues began. Suppressed, unresolved issues and emotions trigger other similar psychological problems, such as chronic anxiety and depression, that feed on each other. In a National Library of Medicine publication, researchers found that emotional instability and the use of expressive suppression might cause state paranoia in psychosis.[29]

Sadly, the positivity movement has been bastardized, and this poses a significant risk to a person's mental health and, ultimately their physical health because they aren't looking under the hood to see what's really going on there.

Their denial that there is a problem *is* the problem.

People can deny a problem exists until they are blue in the face, but the pain will not disappear. It only creates resistance within the body because they aren't validating their lived experiences. Instead, they try to hide them, which feeds further the shame that they aren't capable of willing themselves into happiness or positivity, mistakenly believing that everyone else can and is. This shame of vulnerability keeps emotions hidden and prevents people from developing truly authentic relationships- with others, but most importantly, with themselves. They're afraid people will see their pain, failures, or their perceived inadequacies. They fear being exposed, that others will find out that they don't actually have it all together, don't have all the answers, and aren't as happy as they pretend to be. They're afraid of being judged or, worse,

29   https://pubmed.ncbi.nlm.nih.gov/29460461/

being rejected. Toxic positivity breeds shame, and shame breeds disconnection from the soul.

Suffering is necessary and good for us because it's not just about reaching your goal; it's about the process that really opens you up with all the bumps and bruises. You feel so much more victorious with bumps and bruises. Imagine growing your own vegetables from seeds, being on your knees in the dirt and mud, feeling the earth between your fingers, burying that seed, patiently watering it, and watching the painstakingly slow process of going from seed to seedling to plant. When it comes time to pick and cook your vegetables, they will be the most delicious food you've ever had. The process, patience, and sometimes the struggle make the final product much sweeter. The process itself is nourishment for the soul.

"Everything worthwhile in life is won through surmounting the associated negative experience. Any attempt to escape the negative, to avoid it or quash it or silence it, only backfires. The avoidance of suffering is a form of suffering. The avoidance of struggle is a struggle. The denial of failure is a failure. Hiding what is shameful is itself a form of shame."
- **Mark Manson,** The Subtle Art of Not Giving a F*ck: A Counterintuitive Approach to Living a Good Life

Impact on others

Toxic positivity is dismissive; it devalues and invalidates other people's feelings or experiences. It's not supportive-it's the opposite of emotional intelligence. You may believe you are self-aware, but you aren't aware that you are being toxically positive and possibly extremely annoying, which can be your blind spot. It can stem from either:

- a need to feel in control,
- fear of accepting that life may not be as safe and secure as you would like to believe,
- acknowledging someone else's pain means accepting your own.

When toxic positivity is avoidant, like when you go out of your way to avoid someone who may look gloomy, it is often rooted in fear. Avoidance doesn't solve your problems. It makes them worse. In fact, it may even force colleagues, spouses, employees, friends, and your children to shut down and withdraw from you, fearing your disapproval of their suffering and interpreting it as their inability to choose happiness or overcome their pain. It serves no one, least of all you. When you create this level of damage to the people in your life, it is time to wake up and smell the coffee. Even if your intent is good, intentions don't prevent the negative impact your attitude can have on others.

It gets tricky with children. If you are a parent, there is a common tendency to try to cheer up your child as quickly as possible because you don't want to see them sad or in pain. This can look like words such as, "You're Ok" or "It's not a big deal". Or it could sound like "Stop crying, boys don't cry," or "You have to be tough" or even shaming them. All of these can have a long-term negative impact on their development and ability to express emotions and develop relationships. There is a big difference between teaching them resilience and teaching them that it is not good to show emotions.

Disney Pixar's movie Inside Out captures the importance of honoring our emotions and avoiding minimizing or dismissing them. Parents don't wish their kids to be anything but happy, and that's normal. However, we tell our kids not to be sad and try to distract them or buy them a toy to compensate for their feelings. A better approach is to show empathy and tell them that you understand why they are sad and that feeling sad is a normal human emotion and teach them strategies to cope with it until it passes or to heal it. It is best to teach their children not to be afraid of emotions or not to label them as good or bad, then to find ways to address them productively and healthily.

Life is complex enough that it is not difficult to slip into habits that don't serve us. To err is human. We must be vigilant and realize that we may be harming our relationships and not know it. So, how can you tell? Dr.

Jamie Long of The Psychology Group suggests you look for these signs:

1. Hiding or masking your true feelings
2. Trying to "just get on with it" by dismissing an emotion(s)
3. Feeling guilty for feeling what you feel
4. Minimizing other people's experiences with "feel good" quotes or statements
5. Trying to give someone perspective – "it could be worse" instead of validating their emotional experience
6. Shaming or chastising others for expressing frustration or anything other than positivity
7. Brushing off things bothering you with an "It is what it is"

Acceptance: Emotions are something you have, not who you are. What if you just accepted your emotional suffering for what it is instead of avoiding it? What if you just accepted who you are and what you are feeling now? What if this is the real truth? Having pain in your life doesn't stop you from living. Like being a recovering addict or having lost a limb- these don't change the truth that you are still alive and can still accomplish great things. Toxic positivity damages your attempts to try to live your life with acceptance.

'If you don't accept yourself, how do you expect others to accept you?'

Increasing your self-awareness is an excellent first step to achieving acceptance. If you notice that you may have been pushing the rose-colored glasses a bit too much, practice being mindful of your current emotional state. Notice what's going on in your body and mind. Being mindful is all about taking a mental note of your emotional state. If you notice something negative, don't judge yourself; simply make a note of it, label it as 'emotion' or 'thought', and move on. Dr. Kirkland regularly teaches a happiness psychology class for her undergraduate students. She emphasizes that true happiness does not come from suppressing uncomfortable emotions. She posits that you can't selectively suppress some emotions without suppressing others. The brain does not work that way. This is why I stress that there is no such thing as good and bad emotions. Those descriptions are overgeneralized interpretations of how a person feels. Emotions provide information with a purpose, like signalling a potential threat or fostering a connection. True happiness comes from being more in touch with your emotions and knowing yourself better.

Emotional Intelligence- Back to the self: Achieving self-acceptance takes more than just practicing mindfulness and capturing that information. This is where emotional intelligence comes in. Emotional intelligence, also referred to as emotional quotient (EQ), is the ability to understand one's own and other people's emotions in the decision-making process. It is critical in facilitating high levels of collaboration and productivity, leading to superior performance in the workplace and personal relationships. EQ can be measured with neuroscience-based tools to determine your level of self-awareness, self-regulation, social awareness, social regulation, and intrinsic motivation. Understanding your baseline score empowers you with valuable insights that help guide a path and prioritize a starting point. Ideally, you would do this with a trained and certified EQ expert to provide the techniques to aid the process.

Let's talk about the EQ elephant in the room. On the one hand, everyone knows or has heard of emotional intelligence. On the other, everyone thinks they know about emotional intelligence. Most people think it is about being nice. This cannot be further from the truth. Companies worldwide are in desperate need of EQ training for their leadership. It starts with measuring each leader's EQ using only neuroscience-based EQ assessments that are 100% bias-free and provided by a certified EQ professional. The diagnostic results are up to 95% accurate. Insist on no less from assessment providers. The assessment should also capture blind spots because you can't fix what you can't see. Once measured, the EQ expert will train and guide each leader with strategies on where they most need to improve.

The emotions discussed in Chapter 4 are uncomfortable because it is challenging for people to face them and deal with them. That's what my article about getting under the hood addresses- we don't know why we often feel sad or embarrassed; it's not just something you feel for no reason. Ask yourself, What's triggering that emotion? What's underlying that emotion? It could be something from your childhood that you had forgotten about for years, and suddenly, a current, unrelated event has triggered it, and it has started to peek out. Perhaps you did something that reminded you of a memory and the previous emotions that were never fully acknowledged or processed.

Toxic positivity can be completely benign and unintentional- it can be the go-to for someone who decides that they want to have a better life for themselves. It's no different from choosing to eat healthily. It can appear benign at first, but it's all about how you express it. You wouldn't be forcing the food you choose to eat down someone else's throat just because it is healthy, but when it comes to the positivity mindset, we think the more we reinforce it, the better. This leads to a brainwashing attitude where you will not dare let anybody trample on your positivity! You can either be blindly or desperately committed. Desperate commitment is running away from something – the avoidance trap relates to lacking EQ in the self-awareness category. Blindly committed relates to lacking EQ in the social awareness category because you are unaware of your negative impact on others.

The impact on the person receiving the toxic positivity can range from slight annoyance to drastic disconnection, depending on that person's emotional state. Toxic positivity can be seen as a form of bullying- pushing against others, concerned only with how you want things to be without caring what they might need. The damage can be significant if a person already has mounting struggles and is subjected to toxic positivity. There is a reason why there are so many incidences of suicide linked with bullying and cyberbullying. Technology allows you to hide your identity. When you have the safety of anonymity, it is easier to be bolder and say what you think without seeing the impact this has on the other person - which can be unbearable. Social media is a never-ending frenzy, and as humans, it's easy to get triggered by it. Toxic positivity can have the same effect.

There is neuroscience backing this up. I love the research from Dr. Lisa Feldman Barret on the function of words. Her research reveals how humans, other mammals, and non-mammals use communication that regulates each other. Whatever form we use to communicate with each other instigates regulation in the other person; there is direct feedback because it is information that your brain is receiving, and your body- your nervous system- reacts to the input. Based on what she shows in the brain scans obtained during her experiment, different parts of our brains are activated when different parts of our bodies do different things, whether by indirect input or direct input, such as what we see, smell, hear, or taste. What is fascinating is that her lab performed studies where the subjects would be lying down, completely still, eyes closed, with no other environmental input except for words played through a speaker. The words are a story about a person who is exhausted after meeting friends after work and now driving home. The only input that the whole body is getting is the words, and just from the words, as the story changes and the driver in the story starts to experience stress from driving, the body shows an elevated heart rate, change in hormones, and breathing, all while the person is lying down.

There is a tremendous amount of power in the words we use, and they are impactful because they affect the wiring of your brain- neurological then turns into physical effects.

The bottom line with communication between humans and ourselves, as it relates to toxic positivity, is that we are not talking about intentionally hurting somebody else; in fact the words will have that power irrespective of whether there is intent or not. This is why I feel that, for the most part, toxic positivity comes from people who are well-intentioned but have an underdeveloped EQ and are not aware of the impact they are having on others- they are not able to adapt and 'read the room' as it were. They will be unintentionally insensitive and dismissive of somebody who is experiencing powerful emotions.

Unintended Consequences

The mindfulness movement is a very well-intentioned culprit in the rise of toxic positivity. Over-served mindfulness practices are often misconstrued by people who didn't understand the Zen of it to begin with. They only apply it as a Band-Aid, and that is an example of the poor execution of its teachings. People misguidedly try to solve an issue they're having with a quick fix or a quick pill that doesn't require the actual work. You cannot become a competitive weightlifter if you only want to be able to look at the weights! You have to do the actual work.

What complicates this even further is that it's happening when we are in this VUCA world I described in Chapter 3. Adding to the VUCA conundrum, future-focused technology trends require good collaboration, which means good communication. Trends show that communication skills have been falling more and more by the wayside because people don't communicate like they used to. We live in a world where what we want is short, quick, shallow communication that is ineffective and limits human connection.

Confidently navigating the future means that if we can get clarity for ourselves, get to know ourselves better, and focus our learning skills on adaptability and EQ, everything else will be easier. Why? Because if you have a highly developed EQ, you will be more successful at collaborating and communicating. The more successful you are at that, the more you can leverage the collective power of people around you. At the same time, you contribute meaningfully to their efforts as well.

A high EQ also reduces the wastage of time spent in conflicts. Conflicts are painful. Take a legal dispute, such as a business contract or a couple getting divorced. This is costly, disruptive, and painful, and the only people who benefit are the lawyers. In terms of adaptability, if you can become agile and have an adaptable mind, you can pick up new skills and see rising trends and what's happening in the VUCA world around you because you have more clarity. You won't carry around vast amounts of stress, so you will be able to learn things faster. You re-energize your brain and body when you allow yourself to enrich your mind rather than pollute it. Positive chemicals flow with less resistance, which means you become healthier, and when you feel better emotionally, you're not surviving on tubs of ice cream! Or anything else that is perceived to reduce or dampen the pain. You will see your pain or others' pain for what it is, acknowledge it rather than deny it, and use compassion and empathy in your response.

People are often so desperate to get rid of the pain that they allow themselves to become comfortably numb. When we're numb to some things, we become numb to everything. We cannot pick and choose our emotions. Psychologist Nick Wignall discusses the traits of emotionally strong people and what they do differently. I've incorporated some of his insights below. Use these to guide you toward building better emotional habits.

Emotionally strong people:

- Know that it's not about controlling the emotion. It's about controlling attention- where we are placing our attention. Remember Margaret Thatcher's quote: *"We are what we think."* If emotions were a person, and you were trying to control them, they would say, *"You're not the boss of me!"*

- Practice compassionate self-talk. They are compassionate with themselves first. For example, if you kick yourself or criticize yourself when you are wrong, it's tough to have compassionate feelings for somebody else. We are consistently engaging in negative self-talk. Primarily, that's because ever since we were children, we've been told not to make mistakes, that the only way you would do well in life is if you get As in school. If you got a C, that meant that there was something wrong with you, so you had to work harder, but maybe that's not where your talent was. Perhaps that's not who you were meant to be. Having self-compassion does not mean you stop being self-disciplined. It means you are not a disciplinarian to punish yourself when you get it wrong. It would be best if you were reasonable, realistic, and compassionate. Practice makes permanence- you get better the more you practice, and life always gives us another chance to do better - *it's called tomorrow.*

- Emotionally strong people focus their decisions on values and not on their feelings. Have you ever bought a piece of clothing and in the store thought, "Oh, this is beautiful!" and then when you get home, you ask yourself, "Why did I buy this?" Or you're wine tasting and think you're tasting the best wine ever, so you buy a whole case. But when you drink it at home, it isn't as good as you recall! That's because your emotions were happy and comfortable at the time - you're socializing, and it felt lovely. But, when you make decisions based on values, such as choosing to eat healthily based on the value of being healthy, you will make better choices for yourself in the long-term, which will help you achieve your goals, not just make you happy at that moment.

- Emotions will lead you astray- that's why there are crimes of passion and defenses of temporary insanity. For example, when children misbehave in a store in front of their parents, and the parents finally lose their temper and tell the children that the Disneyland vacation they have planned for the following week is canceled, this is a clear example of emotions gone astray in the moment! Unless you are truly willing to follow through on that threat, the decision to make it was a poor and misguided choice because it was based on feelings - you got frustrated at the moment. Now you've added the burden of dealing with the ramifications of it to your load. You know there is no way you are going to cancel the vacation, you can't get refunds, and you've taken time off work- so why say it? You also lose credibility with your children, and their brains start forming a pattern that shapes future behaviors.

When my daughter was three, we took her on her first trip to Disneyland. The night before and all the way there, I made it very clear that we would not buy any toys on the first day, and maybe not on the second day, but we would on the third day. From a practical perspective, I didn't want to end up with a horde of toys to carry around, and I didn't want to spend a fortune. We went through the whole first day without a hitch, but then we stopped at one of the stores on our way out to look around. My daughter locked eyes on Duchess, her favorite white cat from the Aristocrats, holding her so lovingly and begging me for it. We were all aware that I had made the rule about the toys. I said to her, "Nikita, we talked about this, remember? We will not be buying any toys on the first or second day. Duchess will still be here when we come back." I asked her to put it back, but she couldn't let go. Inside, it was tearing me apart because any parent wants to see their children happy, but I knew I had to follow through. I asked her again to put it back. As if she were twisting the knife inside me or making a brilliant strategic Hail-Mary move, she gave it to me and said, 'Here, you put it back,' as we stood by the stack of Duchesses. I thanked her and gently put it back. She calmly turned around, got in her stroller, and only then started to cry. I told her that I understood her disappointment and explained the plan in more detail. I said that in order for us to pick the toys she wanted the most, we needed to make a list, and I promised her that on the last day, I would buy her the top toys on her list. The funny thing is, she was calm the next day because she knew she could trust my word as I carried the notepad for her list. So, when she saw something she loved, she would say, "Ok, this goes on the list!" On the third day, she got Duchess!

- Emotionally strong people have healthy boundaries. They develop the courage to tell their boss they're unavailable to stay late or give up their weekend because somebody else didn't plan well. Or say no to their family because they have another financial crisis they're going through based on their poor decisions. You've bailed them out many times before, but you've never been paid back. It is like serving alcohol to an alcoholic, damaging your values and hurting your soul. This happened to me until many times over. It was painful because I had to choose between my values and the idea of turning my back on my siblings only to be later resented for having done well for myself when they didn't. Eventually I learned to set healthy boundaries.

Sometimes, the decisions you have to make based on your values are challenging, but that's what emotional maturity requires. If you don't stand up for our values, we effectively devalue them. It's no wonder people are so lost and unsettled these days- they want to take the easy way out, throwing out their values and losing part of who they are.

Emotionally strong people are able to say no. It is how we align our values with our decisions and the goals we want to achieve. To be clear, I'm not advocating to stop being a team player at work or not helping the people you care about. The difference is about standing up for your values if you've started sacrificing them for your own or someone else's destructive patterns.

The Business and Leadership Angle

I think we can live a much better life if we exercise the lessons from a 2012 article, *'The Disciplined Pursuit of Less',* by Greg McKeown, which I came across in the Harvard Business Review.[30]

---

30   https://hbr.org/2012/08/the-disciplined-pursuit-of-less

McKeown's demonstration of the four-phase paradox of a company also applies 100% to its leaders' decision-making abilities and skills.

Phase 1 – When we achieve clarity of purpose, it leads to success.

Phase 2 – When we have success, it leads to more options and opportunities.

Phase 3 – When we have increased options and opportunities, it leads to diffused efforts.

Phase 4 – Diffused efforts undermine the very clarity that led to our success in the first place.

Apple's corporate culture exemplifies this discipline. Steve Jobs was known to eliminate (say no to) many great ideas so the company could focus on the top one or two they would work on. Another example is Warren Buffet's famous 5/25 rule, which emphasizes that you can't do everything at once. It works because we have many goals in many areas of our lives. The rule calls for writing down your top 25 goals. Each must hold value and/or meaning to make it onto the list and positively impact your future. Then select the top 5 from there and only work on those. You only add a new one to the top 5 when you have achieved one of the top 5. You can't break new ground trying to work on them all the same way you can't hold 25 jobs at once. It is about saying no to the many so that you can allocate all your resources to the top 5 and increase your chances of success. I call these 'needle movers.' You don't do it if they don't move the needle in your business.

Losing clarity happens more often than you think. I experienced this effect first-hand when I founded two nanotech organizations and learned how easily this happens. The more success I experienced, the more opportunities appeared, diluting my focus. The challenge is that it is difficult to see it coming, and the reason discipline is critical.

I see it often in my clients who feel lost or overwhelmed running in circles. It has nothing to do with intellect because they are brilliant. The key is knowing how to identify it. I now teach it as part of my professional and leadership development programs, encouraging students to envision themselves as a company pursuing their desired goals. This type of discipline is challenging but not impossible. When achieved, it is mighty.

"The difference between successful people and really successful people is that really successful people say no to almost everything." – Warren Buffett

In addition to clarity and strategic prioritization, a leader must ensure effective communication because it is essential to collaboration, and collaboration is a top capability necessary in a VUCA world and in becoming future-ready. An undeniable shift is occurring globally, much of which is triggered by a VUCA environment that requires people to understand themselves, others and their organizations better.

Collaboration-driven leaders are an advantage in the workplace. Alternative management systems and new collaboration models have emerged and tested with mixed results, such as self-directed teams called holocracy. A 2018 article from Dice Insights wrote: "Unfortunately, **holacracy just doesn't work**. The Evolutionary Leadership theory posits that large groups aren't effective without leadership, and leaders aren't effective without the ability to manage smaller groups. Holacracy doesn't always work well for larger teams and doesn't allow for easy growth."

Part of the reason holacracy fails is the flip side of the coin: collaboration overload – the villain of collaboration. It is like tasting a great slice of pie and enjoying it, but you're not enjoying it as much by the time you get to the nineteenth slice. Companies that have tried to implement holocracy have stepped away from it, including Zappos, GitHub, and Medium, citing various issues such as difficult to implement, lack of accountability, and lack of focus.

Another leadership mistake is thinking that always being optimistic is going to inspire your team to be optimistic and happy. This is not the case. Liz Wiseman, the author of the best-selling book *Multipliers*, describes the actions that make a leader a multiplier or a diminisher. Diminishers suffocate their people, but they are usually not doing it on purpose or even unaware of it. In the case of always being optimistic, the leader diminishes the people around them because they don't feel they're being heard. Always being optimistic doesn't leave room for anyone else to express themselves or their ideas or show the leader is not in tune with the workplace.

Key takeaway: EQ helps prevent the bad habit of toxic positivity in the workplace or your personal life. It is never about your intentions but about the other person being heard and validated. Improving your EQ will help you connect with others and achieve effective communication, which is vital to becoming future-ready.

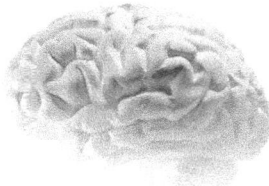

CHAPTER 6

THE DARK SIDE OF INNOVATION (FUTURE-READINESS)

We live in a globally connected world, and that's good. Collaboration tools allow us to connect with people worldwide. The problem is that our society has commoditized human connection. Everything else has become more important because we are so connected that there are many more demands on families and working professionals today. It used to be that if you were a bookkeeper, you just had to know how to do basic bookkeeping. If you were a mechanic, cars were easy to understand. Now, everything is a lot more complex, hence VUCA. As complexity grows, so does ambiguity. Access to information explaining how everything works is harder to find, thus creating more uncertainty. The volatility, the whirlwind around everything else – our lives and our businesses – makes it nearly impossible to prioritize effective communication and make real human connections. There's just no time, so we fall into the trap of constant urgency, where we develop faulty behavior and decision-making patterns because we're constantly trying to keep up. Think about it this way. You are late to an unfamiliar destination and have no GPS (your phone battery is dead), but you have the street name for your turn. If you are driving 60 MPH (not recommended except where allowed), you can't expect to read every street name you pass, can you? This pattern does not set you up for success, yet I see this behavioral mindset applied to business and personal decisions more often than I'd like.

I don't believe humans want to go that fast, but you can count on this – technology will never be slower than it is today, and it was never slower than five or ten years ago. We fool ourselves by believing this spike is temporary, but that is never the case. I know this well because I've run this race many times. In the last three decades, we have seen global technological races for dominance in game-changing technologies. For example, after the Space Race of the 1960s, we didn't see a concentrated global race until the 1990s. First, there was a race for online dominance with the rise of the Internet. The search for the killer app on smartphones began at the turn of the century. The race for nanotechnology was in the same decade, followed by the human genome race. Now, major countries are in a race for intelligence – artificial intelligence (AI). Timelines are compressing, and significant technological revolutions are coming faster and faster. Each innovation triggers convergent exponential technologies. Exponential Technologies are technologies that are doubling and recombining, giving birth to game-changing innovations like:

Exponential Technologies

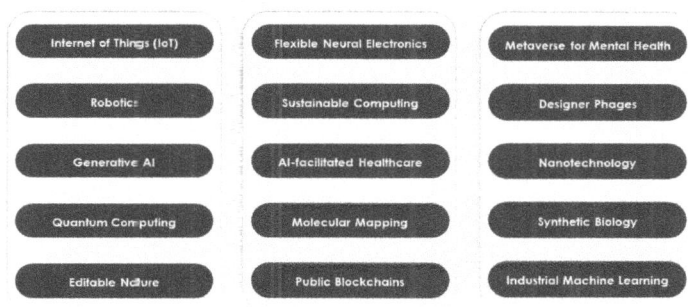

Internet of Things (IoT)	Flexible Neural Electronics	Metaverse for Mental Health
Robotics	Sustainable Computing	Designer Phages
Generative AI	AI-facilitated Healthcare	Nanotechnology
Quantum Computing	Molecular Mapping	Synthetic Biology
Editable Nature	Public Blockchains	Industrial Machine Learning

The issue is that humans are trying to keep up but can't. Extensive research from MIT's Erik Brynjolfsson and Andrew McAfee snows, beyond a reasonable doubt, that technological progress eliminates jobs and leaves average workers worse off than they were before. They call this the 'great decoupling.'[31]

They state: Innovation has never been faster, and yet at the same time, we have a falling median income, and we have fewer jobs. People are falling behind because technology is advancing so fast, and our skills and organizations aren't keeping up.

---

31   https://hbr.org/2015/06/the-great-decoupling

I'm very grateful to have amassed a multidisciplinary, multifunctional, and multi-industry background that has kept me at the forefront of innovation. For three decades, I've been an ardent observer of technology and behavioral trends that began with a deep understanding of the technology adoption lifecycle, mostly tracking and studying the impact of disruption on businesses and leaders and investigating innovative ways to get ahead of the problems caused by disruptions.

Ultimately, as individuals, whether you're a leader or a manager or a professional, what impacts your life impacts your business, and what disrupts your business also disrupts your life because we're human beings- we feel it. From a brain science perspective, I enjoy helping companies and leaders redefine what's possible for them while making it a fun experience.

We've been rolling out disruptive innovations for centuries and experienced many industrial revolutions well before the 'disruptive innovations' term existed. It is a testament to the power and spirit of human ingenuity and the need to solve problems.

In a popular TEDxBerkely Talk entitled 'The Art of Innovation,' Guy Kawasaki describes the evolution of the ice business in the late 1800s and what was required to be in that business.[32] You had to live in a cold place where you would harvest the ice from frozen lakes and ponds

---

32   https://www.youtube.com/watch?v=Mtjatz9r-Vc

and then deliver it by horse. The only way to expand was with more horses, but this was not innovative but rather duplicative. In the 1900s, 9 million pounds of ice were harvested. Let's refer to this as Ice 1.0. Thirty years later, ice factories appeared where ice was 'made', meaning ice only needed to be delivered, not harvested – Ice 2.0.

Another 30 years later, you no longer needed ice delivered because people would have their own 'factory' and make their own ice at home. This was the refrigerator, or Ice 3.0.

Interestingly, none of the previous generations of companies innovated because they only defined themselves by what they did – an ice harvester company, an ice factory, and makers of mechanical ice-making machines.

From this story and the chart below, we can see that with every major passing innovation, the speed of adoption has also accelerated because innovation in one area triggers rapid innovation in other areas. Behaviorally, we are more adept at adopting innovations because we've had more practice coupled with more access to information. This is why Pokemon Go was able to reach 50 million users in 19 days! Disruption is not bad, as long as you can adapt to it.[33] Observations like these prepared me to look at my nanotechnology research from a big-picture perspective, not just a single application perspective.

---

33   https://www.visualcapitalist.com/how-long-does-it-take-to-hit-50-million-users

Behavioral Technology Adoption

Product or Technology	Year Launched	Time to 50 Million Users
Airlines	1914	64 years
Automobiles	1886	62 years
Telephone	1877	50 years
Electricity	1925	46 years
Credit Cards	1958	28 years
Television	1927	22 years
ATMs	1967	18 years

Product or Technology	Year Launched	Time to 50 Million Users
Computers	1977	14 years
Mobile Phones	1981	12 years
Internet	1993	7 years
Facebook	2004	4 years
WeChat	2011	1 year
Pokémon Go	2016	19 days
ChatGPT	2022	5 days

I updated this chart with ChatGPT, which only took five days to reach 50 million users. I love being on the disrupting side and have enjoyed working, collaborating, or advising several start-ups on their disruptive innovations. Of course, when you are the one being disrupted, it is no fun at all!

The lesson about disruption is that if the incumbents don't move fast enough or aren't paying attention, they're going to get disrupted. Many companies started ousting their CEOs in 2018 because they missed major disruptive trends that were happening. Most commonly, the disruptors are the new cool-kid start-ups. In rare cases, some enterprises genuinely reinvent themselves from the inside out when they spot disruptive trends and actively work to stay ahead of the pack. If they don't, you'll find plenty of examples where CEOs were ousted, such as Blockbuster Video, Barnes & Noble (twice), Victoria's

Secret, IBM, Toys R Us, Ford, GE, J CREW, Mattress Firm, Mattel, and others.[34]

Disruptive Technologies

Renowned Harvard Business School professor Clayton Christensen first wrote about disruptive technology and innovation in the 90s, describing it as when one technology displaces an established technology and changes the nature or structure of an industry.

In short, disruptive technologies force companies to alter how they do business lest they become obsolete, sometimes quite quickly.

These technologies also give way to new opportunities that accelerate progress in other areas. For example, quantum computing appears to be coming of age. While there are still hurdles to overcome, emerging innovation use cases are growing. These include enhanced artificial intelligence and machine learning, solutions for climate change, clean energy and sustainability, R&D for Pharmaceuticals and Chemicals, manufacturing to supply chains, and financial modeling.

My overarching goal for this chapter is to provoke thought and discussion centered on future readiness. I want people to be thinking about it and what it might mean to them and those around them.

---

34   CB Insights Research.

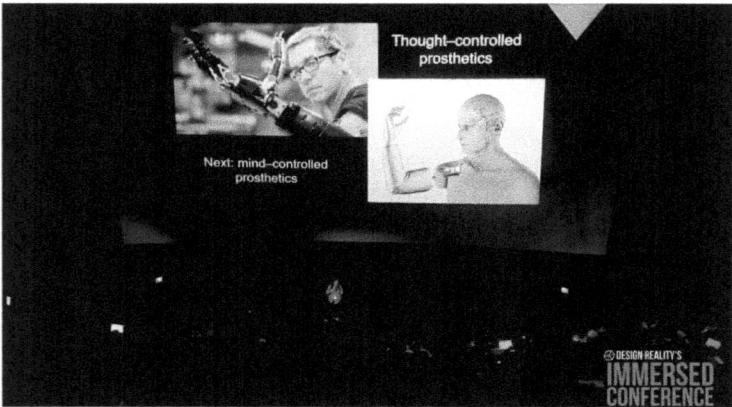

Here are just a few technologies I have presented on that even recently were considered futuristic:

1. **Thought-controlled prosthetics** – wired directly to the brain. Next up: spine-controlled prosthetics, allowing them to feel.

2. **Cars** –forget self-driving. The number of eVTOL (electric vertical take-off and landing) and aerial vehicle manufacturers have been growing significantly to about 200, including companies that provide sustainable intercity travel and flying taxi services such as SkyDrive and Uber Air.

3. **Quantum Computing** – has undoubtedly emerged as a groundbreaking field of research and innovation promising seismic impact, revolutionizing how we solve complex problems and opening new fields of discovery previously deemed impossible for classical computers. It can

potentially force the largest technology upgrade cycle in computer history.

4. **Drone Bees and Dragon Fly Cyborg**- as artificial pollinators to address the bee shortage.

5. **3D Printing** – anything from an acoustic guitar to artificial organs...

6. **AI, Machine Learning/Deep Learning–** ranging from healthcare innovation and linking humans to AI for knowledge management to deep fakes distorting digital reality, and more sophisticated cyberattacks.

The PGP Loop - Problems that every leader encounters

"The gap between 'sci-fi'- that which was once imagined- and 'sci-fact'- that which becomes manifest and real, is shrinking." Josh Wolfe, Co-founder and Managing Partner, Lux Capital

We live in a world of unprecedented uncertainty, but the good news is that this gives us unparalleled opportunities – if you are paying attention. With disruptive and exponential technologies, the pace and magnitude of change demands more from leaders and their teams when trying to compete and avoid becoming obsolete. In many ways, it creates the proverbial hamster wheel that keeps you stuck and unable to keep up, giving way to sacrificing other important areas in your life.

It's not a pretty picture. Imagine waking up one day to a looming threat of potentially becoming obsolete. The psychological and cognitive impact is significant as an overwhelming wave of emotions takes over. In this situation, the objectivity needed for smart decision-making will depend on how resilient and emotionally fit you are. The two most fundamental and critical skills for success include systems thinking and emotional intelligence.

Systems Thinking

Systems thinking is a way of making sense of the world's complexity by looking at the whole and relationship rather than breaking it down into parts. It is a holistic approach to analyzing situations and, with mastery, even getting ahead of new disruptions

Emotional Intelligence

Emotional intelligence is the ability to identify and regulate one's own emotions, as well as the emotions of others. Awareness and regulation of emotions are vital to harnessing and applying them to strategic thinking and problem-solving.

In a world of constant transformation, becoming future-ready is critical. The notion that you either keep up or get pushed out is overwhelming. Prolonged states in what I call the 'PGP Loop' – Pace, Gaps, Priorities Loop – are unsustainable in the long run.

PGP LOOP

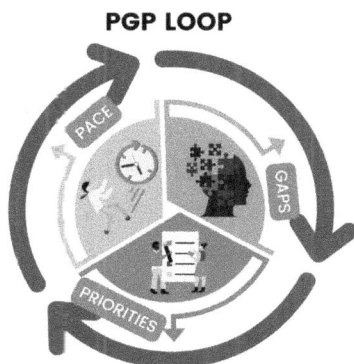

1. **Pace** - Innovation has never been faster, and yet at the same time, people have a falling median income, and there are fewer jobs or people with the right skills. *"The Great Decoupling"* I mentioned earlier discusses how technological advances impact our society. People are falling behind because technology is advancing rapidly, and our skils and organizations aren't keeping up. It leads to unrest, despair, and overwhelm, which decreases productivity and the ability to stay competitive. It also increases stress and workplace conflict, which affects leaders professionally and personally.

2. **Gaps** – The innovation pace directly affects leaders' ability to become adaptable and invest in themselves to develop and sharpen their skills. When times change, using outdated and ineffective leadership tools and models only creates more

problems. The magnitude, pace, and breadth of demands require more time, making time more and more scarce. Unsurprisingly, CEOs, senior executives, and board members consistently cite the top human performance soft skills that impact the bottom line and that they represent current gaps. These include:

a. Social skills – Communication and relationship-building skills
b. Leadership/Delegation skills
c. People-oriented problem solving - conflict management and listening skills
d. Adaptability and resilience skills
e. Organizational alignment - mentoring/developing talent skills

These gaps have a negative multiplier effect throughout the organization, including higher turnover rates, lower employee morale, lack of accountability, and higher incidents of unresolved conflict in the workplace.[35]

3. **Priorities** - With disadvantages in crucial skills and the struggle of navigating a world at the speed of change where everything is a moving target,

---

[35] Harvard Business Review "The C-Suite Skills That Matter Most" https://hbr.org/2022/07/the-c-suite-skills-that-matter-most and Gartner Group "Top 10 Emerging Skills For The C-Suite" https://www.gartner.com/smarterwithgartner/top-10-emerging-skills-for-the-c-suite

it is no wonder that the availability of time has become a scarce commodity. 22% of the leaders surveyed said time was their greatest challenge. Time was especially problematic for members of the Forbes Communications Council (36%) and Forbes Finance Council (33%), leaders just below the C-suite in VP positions (29%), and financial services professionals (42%).[36] There are only two choices – do nothing and stay in the loop or do something about it. I propose that while the root cause of this PGP problem loop may be #1-Pace, investing in yourself and your leadership team (#2-Gaps) will eliminate a lot of the time wastage from being ineffective at leadership and delegation, and conflict management, listening, mentoring, and developing talent and communication. The primary point here is to prioritize effectiveness, not efficiency. With efficiency, you get to do more, faster. With effectiveness, you get to do less but better, which protects your most valuable asset – your time.

Without intelligent prioritization and understanding of your values, skills gaps, and pace, the PGP Loop problem snowballs. The scary question is: How can we be future-ready if we aren't even present-ready? This is already happening at all levels of leadership because it filters down from the top. Leaders must understand the impact

---

36   Forbes Council https://forbescouncils.com/2018/10/top-5-exec-utive-challenges/

they have on their employees and their ability to perform their best work.

AI – The Race for Intelligence

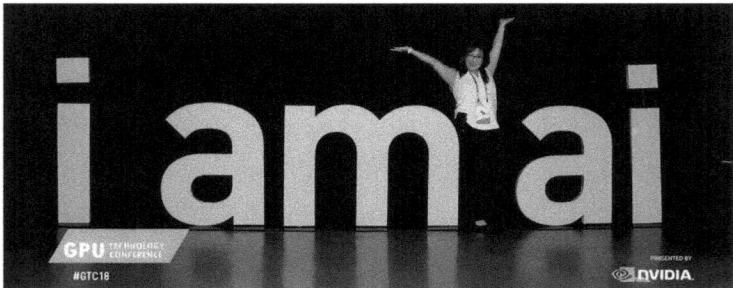

Me at the NVIDIA GPU Conference.

Earlier in this chapter, I mentioned previous global technology races such as the global Space Race of the 60s, the Human Genome race of the 90s completed in 2003, and the nanotechnology race at the turn of the century with the signing of the NNI (National Nanotechnology Initiative) initiated by President Bill Clinton and signed by President George W. Bush in 2003. The convergence of Big Data and Processing Power has ushered in a new race, the *race for intelligence*, which makes AI and machine learning possible.

AI continues to grow exponentially in capabilities fueled by huge spikes in start-ups and investments. Before the pandemic, record funding to AI startups reached $31.1 billion and 2200 deals worldwide in 2019. By comparison, in 2018 we saw $22.1B invested across 1900 deals and

$16.8 billion across 1700 deals in 2017. Normalizing over a 5-year period, I saw the same growth in the number of deals but higher investment on a per-deal basis. The pandemic only flattened AI investment in 2020 to $32.5 billion but it spiked to $72.1 billion in 2021.

The possibility of enabling products that are sometimes controversial and sometimes concerning exists, such as deepfake technologies, and we must determine how to address this. One example is the company Synthesia, which can take a celebrity's face and mold it to look like it's natively speaking in other languages. We are seeing more celebrities like Tom Hanks and the late Robin Williams' daughter, Zelda Williams, speak up against this. Companies can acquire and exploit this technology, which can already be seen in political videos and morphed pornography. The technology can replicate anyone, dead or alive, and it can look authentic. While AI offers excellent opportunities for creativity and innovation, it also raises ethical and legal dilemmas about consent, authenticity, and the potential for misuse.

It's not just the new startups that are leveraging AI; the larger, more prominent companies are also acquiring this technology to avoid falling behind. Companies such as Walmart filed six AI patents in 2017 for autonomous robot bees using AI-powered cameras to prevent theft at checkout lanes. A VP at Microsoft demonstrated a live image of herself speaking in full Japanese, real-time, in a

2019 meeting with clients in Japan- and she doesn't speak Japanese!

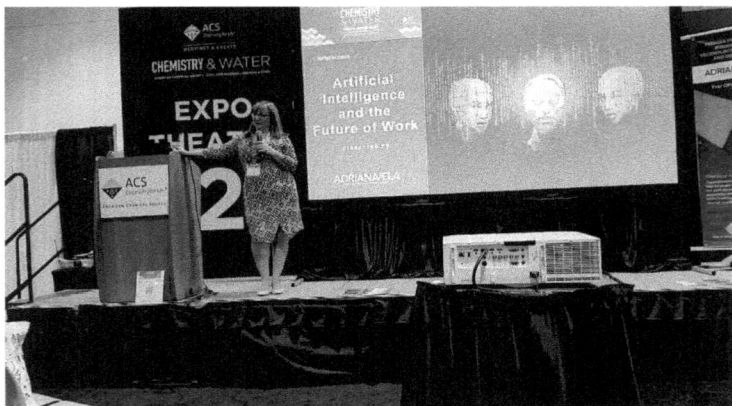

Presenting on AI and the Future of Work at the 2019 American Chemical Society Conference.

Big tech FAMGA – Facebook, Amazon, Microsoft, Google, and Apple are making big bets on AI. A research report from CBInsights shows the number of AI companies acquired between 2010 and 2021 and who has been leading the AI race.[37] Among FAMGA, Apple leads the way. With 29 total disclosed AI acquisitions since 2010, the company has made nearly twice as many acquisitions as second-place Google (the frontrunner from 2012 to 2016), with 15 acquisitions.

Microsoft follows Apple and Google with 13 acquisitions, Facebook with 12, and Amazon with 7. Many of FAMGA's

37 https://www.cbinsights.com/research/apple-leads-artificial-in-telligence-acquisitions/

prominent products and services — such as Apple's Siri or Google's contributions to healthcare through DeepMind — came out of acquisitions of AI companies.

Which future would you choose?

Technology makes life easier in many ways, but who governs these technologies? Price Waterhouse Coopers published a report on the workforce of the future and the competing forces shaping 2030.[38] The report describes four possible worlds of work depending on which competing forces dominate. All four are possible based on trends, patterns, and behaviors. People can't afford to be a passenger in the future or fall asleep at the wheel because they may not like what they see when they wake up. Take a moment to imagine these four worlds and what they mean to you.

1. **The Red World** is the perfect incubator for innovation. Anything that we can think we want to do, we can do, with organizations and individuals racing to give consumers what they want. Digital platforms and technology enable those with winning ideas and specialist and niche profit markets to flourish. Businesses innovate to create personalization and find new ways to serve these niches. New products and business models can

---

38   https://www.pwc.com/gx/en/services/people-organisation/
publications/workforce-of-the-future.html

be developed at lightning speed, powered by technology and big data.

Organizations are stripped down and nimble with no separate HR function because they mostly use outsourced specialists for the duration of the project or entire business as they move on to other hot ideas. But the risks could be high in a world where ideas rule, and innovation outpaces regulation. Today's winning business could be tomorrow's court case or nightmare in this Red World scenario.

2. **The Blue World** is where the big corporations are kings- bigger *is* better. Organizations see their size and influence as the best way to protect their profit margins against fierce competition from their peers and aggressive new market entrants. Corporations grow to such a scale and exert such influence that some become more powerful and larger than national economies. It's a world where individual preferences take precedence over social responsibility.

Through the use of physical and medical enhancements, including the brain, it is a world of extreme talent where exceptional people are in high demand. Workplace performance is pushed to its limits through automation, analytics, and innovation. Workers' performance is continually measured and analyzed, enabling a new breed of elite super-workers.

3. **The Green World** is where corporate responsibility is the priority. It's characterized by a strong social conscience, a sense of environmental responsibility, a focus on diversity and human rights, and a recognition that business has an impact beyond the financial. In a Green World, workers and consumers demand that organizations do right by their employees and the wider world. Trust is the basic currency underpinning business and employment. Companies must place their societal purpose at the heart of their commercial strategy.

From the workforce perspective, employees will be attracted to companies they admire, and they will have two to three weeks of paid leave just to do social or charitable work, but workers have to pledge to reflect the company's work values at work and home. The HR function has a much higher position in the Green World, renamed 'People and Society,' and the idea of a job for life actually returns.

From a technology perspective, we consumers wouldn't have all the gadgets we want. Technology is only developed to protect resources and environmental damage. It would also be used extensively to replace travel because of the impact travel has on the environment. In a Green World, humans pay the cost for the companies to meet their ethical and environmental goals.

4. **The Yellow World** is where humans come first, where workers and companies seek more significant meaning and relevance in what they do. Social-first and community businesses find the greatest success and prosper. Crowdfunded capital flows towards ethical and blameless brands. It's a world where workers and consumers search for meaning and relevance from organizations with a social heart. Where artisans, makers, and 'new Worker Guilds' thrive, and humanness is highly valued.

   But there are also negatives. There won't be a diversity of skills in the workforce because like-minded workers gravitate toward each other through technology. Collaboration is key for working on projects and ideas, which you won't have without diversity, and guilds will help create scale and build trust, which means only the members are protected- as with a union. In a Green World, the work is fluid and unstructured, and the work/home borders are blurred.

   There is a massive conflict regarding technology in the Yellow World which calls for it to only be used for back-office functional support- automation of tasks that are impossible for humans and not for convenience. It's not about making human lives better; as long as there are humans who can do the work, that's who will do the work.

Try this: now that you've read the description of the four possible worlds of work, reflect and answer the following questions:

- What world would you prefer to have? Why?
- Which world would you dislike the most? Why?
- Which one do you think will most likely dominate? Why?
- Which one are you honestly contributing to the most? In what way?
- Did you always feel this way, or has your preference changed? What caused the change?

As a reminder, there are no right or wrong answers, but answering them honestly and authentically will provide insights about yourself and your values. What will you prioritize? What are you willing to give up, and for what?

Sticky issues about the fast-moving innovation train: The regulation dilemma

Earlier, I talked about the 'race for intelligence.' Like the nanotechnology race, there is a lot of hype and a lot of promise. As a systems thinker, I carefully reflect on how technology shapes us. In a talk I gave entitled '*Technology*

Convergence – Shaping the Technologies That Shape Us, I promoted that we need to *think before we tech.* And that we have a moral obligation to follow and understand the basics of emerging technologies and their impact on society to shape the technologies that shape us.

I'm a big fan of technology. In fact, I ranked in the top 2% of innovation-driven future-thinking professionals out of more than six million participants assessed. This was my first introduction to the talent diagnostics tools I licensed because they are neuroscience-validated, backed by 35 years of research, and 100% bias-free. It is why I'm an ardent observer of behaviors and technology trends.

When it comes to technology regulation, the deep questions I ponder give me pause.

i. To regulate or not to regulate, that is the question?
ii. Are regulatory agencies up to the task?
iii. Should regulation be the cart or the horse? In other words, should we have the regulation before it's fully mainstreamed?

This isn't my first rodeo. I've been down this road many times during my ten years spent exclusively on nanotechnologies. Because part of my mission for NanoBioNexus was to promote the safe commercialization of nanotechnologies applied to diagnostics, therapeutics, and medical devices, I was in tune with the Federal Drug Administration's (FDA's) forming of a Task Force in 2006.

I spoke with many FDA Task Force members determining regulatory approaches that encouraged the continued development of innovative, safe, and effective FDA-regulated products that use nanotechnology materials.

The benefit of having meaningful conversations resulted in a deep appreciation for the challenge and pressure mounted on the FDA to publish industry guidance. Understandably, the fast pace of a research-driven innovation pipeline that needed approval grew because of the need to reduce the pain and suffering from diseases like cancer. Advances include significantly reducing the side effects of most cancer therapeutics, monitoring, and early detection approaches.

As a result of my organization's efforts and contributions to advances in nanobiotechnologies through our partnership with the University of CA, San Diego, and the National Cancer Institute-funded Nano-Tumor Center, I was invited to opine on the 2014 FDA set of guidelines published in an article from Wolters Kluwer.[39]

The FDA's stance and summary of its efforts continue. As of 2018, the positioning and commitment is:[40]

"As a public health agency using scientific information to make regulatory decisions about products ranging from

39   https://adrianavela.expert/strategic-perspectives-tiny-particles-with-big-implications-nanotechnology-and-the-fda/
40   https://www.fda.gov/science-research/nanotechnology-programs-fda/fdas-approach-regulation-nanotechnology-products

cosmetics to chemotherapy agents to food packaging, the FDA has long encountered the combination of promise, risk, and uncertainty that accompanies emerging technologies. Nanotechnology is not unique in this regard. Materials can exhibit new or altered physicochemical properties at nanoscale dimensions, enabling novel product development. However, the changes in biological, chemical, and other properties that can make nanotechnology applications so exciting may also merit examination to determine any effects on product safety, effectiveness, or other attributes."

Another area of regulation that I educated myself on was that of the Center for Disease Control's (CDC) National Institute for Occupational Safety and Health (NIOSH) and its Nanotechnology Research Center (NTRC), which leads the federal government in research focused on developing the guidance on the occupational safety and health implications and applications of advanced manufacturing, including nanomaterial manufacturing.[41] I read their reports and contacted some authors to interview them and get more insights into the risks' inherent issues, the implications, and compliance.

The point of my sharing previous insights and lessons learned is because the topic of regulation on emerging technologies remains relevant and, in many ways, even more elusive when it comes to AI. In the February 2020

---

41   https://www.cdc.gov/niosh/programs/nano/default.html

VentureBeat article, Alphabet CEO Sundar Pichai called AI *"more profound than fire or electricity."*[42]

The article also cites that not all governments agree on the topic of regulation. The U.S. government is taking a hands-off approach. The EU is taking bigger steps toward regulation, and leaders in the AI space have stated their positions with the European Commission advising they take a proportionate or light-touch approach.

From my perspective, is the U.S. showing signs of facing the reality that regulating AI would be like pushing a rope, given society's behavioral trends of the undisciplined pursuit of more? I've never claimed the title of 'Futurist,' even if I've been called that, but for many decades, I've developed and tuned my ability to connect dots, the confidence to be comfortable with disruption and to examine my own biases. It has served me well and guided my career trajectory and research focus. I am where I need to be, doing what I know needs to be done. Are you where you need to be? Are you living the life you want and deserve?

What can you do? Wake up and level up... but with eyes wide open.

Let's not forget: technology is selfish. It waits for no one.

---

42 https://venturebeat.com/2020/02/01/why-were-failing-to-regu-late-the-most-powerful-tech-weve-ever-faced/

Do I remain a technology catalyst despite the dark side of innovation? Yes, absolutely, but I do so with eyes wide open, and I hope you will, too. I don't blindly drink the Kool-Aid. I use systems thinking and the strength of knowing myself to make my own decisions, carve my own path, and not succumb to groupthink.

Systems thinking comes in as we consider various trends that may not appear interconnected but are. Even before the COVID-19 pandemic, society already found itself overwhelmed by all the distractions and disruptions and had no time to invest in core self-development. Increases in distractions like millions of promotional content, apps, and video clips eat up learning and personal or professional development time. But that's not all. Learners have become more impatient as they struggle to concentrate and be productive. The average employee experiences as many as sixty distractions and three to four interruptions daily.[43]

The top five workplace distractions include:

1. Talkative coworkers – 80%
2. Workplace noise – 70%
3. Overwhelm by new changes – 61%
4. Meetings – 60%
5. Social media – 56%

---

43   17 Concerning Workplace Distraction Statistics [2022]: Facts + Trends - Zippia For Employers https://www.zippia.com/employer/workplace-distraction-statistics/

Now add on top of these major disruptions like the global pandemic and its economic, health, and emotional impact, including the impact from civil unrest in the U.S. and other countries and you have a mental health crisis in your hands.

From a brain science perspective, the implications of this data are alarming, and it is no surprise we are not where we should be relative to the fast pace of innovation. We continue to lose ground, and the more ground we lose, the worse we feel about where we are and the more inadequate, un-confident, and ill-equipped we feel about ourselves and our abilities to handle the future. The reality is concerning enough that some may fall into quiet despair. If not, they live a lie and are in denial just to get by. But there is a way out. I call it becoming *VUCA resilient*. Throughout this book, I provide many nuggets that improve your odds of getting ahead. They may not appear directly connected, but that's only because you've not yet mastered systems thinking.

Innovation comes from observations, but success comes from communication.

In the 1840s, Dr. Ignaz Semmelweis, an Austrian physician, made an interesting observation that when doctors washed their hands before treating patients with puerperal fever, the death rate fell tenfold. He shared his findings with colleagues and proposed handwashing as a standard practice. Despite the data, other doctors dismissed the findings. His colleagues and even his own wife thought he had lost his mind and committed him to an asylum, where he died shortly after.

The mental model of disease in 1840 was an imbalance of four humors in the body: phlegm, black bile, yellow bile, and blood. It made every disease internal and unique. This is why the doctors could not see how an external action would affect the person's health.

So why did Louis Pasteur succeed a few decades later when Semmelweis failed? Pasteur proved that germs were the primary cause of disease, which triggered a new mental model where doctors could understand how handwashing would affect health, making personal hygiene a new standard of care.

The lesson from this story is that shifts in thinking within the existing mental model only serve to challenge that model, and that challenge creates resistance and a negative response. This lesson applies to many things; when you think in a certain way or have certain beliefs that blind you to other possibilities, you could be missing so much, and you typically are. It is the reason some people don't adapt. An old saying comes to mind: *"A man convinced against his will is of the same opinion still."* Innovation requires adaptation. Without adaptability skills, you simply become a victim of VUCA instead of capitalizing on new opportunities.

Have you ever wondered why, even today, there is so much resistance to the idea of changing or adapting one's beliefs? Humans are attached to the idea of being right, but it's not always ego-driven; it's what we have been taught from grade school up to 'defending' your PhD thesis. Interesting choice of words, 'defending.'

"I LOVE, LOVE, LOVE being wrong because I learned something new each time."

This has been my philosophy from a young age because starting with nothing made me appreciate having new knowledge that empowered me. Learning something new got me closer to my goal of escaping poverty. It was about learning a better way. I actively sought people who had more experience and knowledge I could learn from. Therefore, when I was 19, all my friends were in their 30s and 40s. Years later as a leader and entrepreneur, I always sought to hire people who I thought were smarter than me or someone with excellent potential and who I could help grow. It is the essence of paying it forward. In fact, I formalized that when I hired interns at my company. I would give them professional development, and they had to create ways to pay it forward to high school students.

Perhaps this is why I find it interesting how people work so hard to be right. What they don't realize is that they let their ego take charge. Recall from Chapter 4 that the ego is not your amigo and seeks to damage your soul. It takes courage to accept being wrong, but you feel the aliveness in your soul during the act of courage. Congratulations if you are one of these people who are comfortable saying this. Celebrate yourself and enjoy the richness of learning, expanding your horizons, and feeding your soul. It means you are open-minded and comfortable with yourself, knowing that if you are wrong, it's not because you're broken. You just hadn't learned that new thing yet. Change your communication with others and yourself, and you change the result.

In Chapter 4, I discussed mental models and provided a few examples. I used this story with every new crop of interns I hired to make the point about how important it is to understand what mental models are in place to determine the best new mental models to apply.

The context of this professional development training I provided to my interns was to think in terms of employing innovative ways to problem-solve on the projects I assigned them, but also to approach their future career choices, taking into account their own mental models at play. Then I'd give examples of how this thinking applied to selling their ideas, inventions, and even themselves as innovators with each career climb.

The underlying concept has not changed. Innovators change the lens through which we see the world. Successful innovative companies understand this well. For example, Steve Jobs championed the mantra "think different" and shifted people's perception of technology as being more personal and an extension of themselves. The company, Salesforce.com, also shifted the paradigm of computing by marketing the idea of "No Software" to reflect the shift from packaged installed software to cloud computing and a SaaS (software-as-a-service) business model. If they had not done this, the customers would not have understood their product's benefits.

This type of thinking is rooted in systems thinking to adopt actionable mental models to apply to your company, your organization, and yourself. It goes way beyond thought leadership. Adopting systems thinking has never been more important than it is today because only then will we start looking at things not just for what they are but for what they could mean.

Future readiness – Why we are falling behind

Our education system is unable to keep up. Not now and not in the foreseeable future. But don't just take it from me. In a McKinsey & Company interview, Andrew Ng comments on how to make the transition into the AI age easier for everyone. Andrew Ng is a globally recognized leader in AI. He is the Founder of DeepLearning.AI, Founder & CEO of Landing AI, General Partner at AI Fund, Chairman & Co-Founder of Coursera, and an Adjunct Professor at Stanford University's Computer Science Department.

Interview transcript

Andrew Ng: AI is the new electricity. About 100 years ago, we started rolling out electricity in the United States, and it changed every single major industry, everything ranging from healthcare and culture to transportation, communications, and manufacturing is now all electrically powered.[44]

---

44 Andrew Ng https://www.mckinsey.com/featured-insights/
future-of-work/the-evolution-of-employment-and-skills-in-the-
age-of-ai

We now see a surprisingly clear path for AI to also transform every single major industry. Everything ranging from much better healthcare to more personalized education to much more efficient retail and manufacturing to self-driving cars. This will displace a lot of jobs, everything ranging from call-center operators to, when self-driving cars come, the millions of truck drivers and maybe taxi drivers whose jobs will be affected. But this is true for white-collar and blue-collar workers.

AI's getting really good at reading radiology images, so if any of you have a son or daughter or a friend graduating from medical school with a radiology degree, I think they might have a perfectly good 5-year career in radiology. Maybe even 10 years. But I wouldn't plan for a 40-year career doing that same radiology job today. This will create challenges and will put pressure on society to figure out solutions such as a new educational system to help those whose jobs will be displaced.

Earlier in this chapter, I mentioned the research about the *'Great Decoupling'* by MIT's McAfee and Brynjolfson, and how people at all levels of their careers are falling behind related to the pace of innovation, including leaders and CEOs. In a VUCA world, you need to develop different skills. Not everyone working on innovation, especially leaders, has the right upskilling and leadership training required. I mentioned some of those skills earlier concerning systems thinking, but here are others:[45]

---

45   Harvard Extension School, 2020.

10 Emerging Skills for Professionals – All Fields

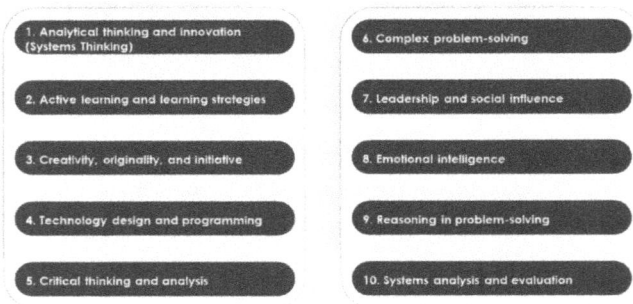

1. Analytical thinking and innovation (Systems Thinking)	6. Complex problem-solving
2. Active learning and learning strategies	7. Leadership and social influence
3. Creativity, originality, and initiative	8. Emotional intelligence
4. Technology design and programming	9. Reasoning in problem-solving
5. Critical thinking and analysis	10. Systems analysis and evaluation

From a brain empowerment perspective, developing foundational brain skills will facilitate progress in other skills development. I discuss these in more detail in Chapter 8.

Fundamental brain development skills you can't do without:

- Adaptability
- Disruption resiliency
- Mental dexterity and resilience
- Emotional Intelligence and resilience

Time to update that leadership playbook

There has been a long-standing success playbook for CEOs that no longer works today. If CEOs want success, their playbook requires a makeover and reprioritization. The first step current and aspiring C-suite executives must take is updating their skills. More importantly, they must accept that gaps exist, and that deep expertise is required to navigate uncertainty and solve complex problems, not just for themselves; their leadership team and employees also need similar training to maintain alignment in the organization. These complex problems draw leaders outside their knowledge and comfort zones. Over the last five to seven years, there has been a noticeable shift in the variety of competencies the role requires. If you want to weather uncertainty and disruptions with resilience, the changes mean you must increase your transformation readiness with dynamic learning. Here are a few CEO-specific skills that should be acquired, updated, or sharpened.

- High tolerance for ambiguity – with the business terrain constantly evolving and VUCA in effect, it is virtually impossible for CEOs to set the path forward when they have no concrete knowledge that allows them to project what their company might look like in 5, 10, or 20 years. It requires becoming comfortable with ambiguity and the capacity to adapt to situations as they change. Being massively adaptable and disciplined in searching for the truth within unknowns will build the confidence you need to increase your tolerance for ambiguity.

- Capacity to understand and embrace new technology – Technology is essential to running businesses and is becoming crucial to enhance their competitive edge. CEOs must understand or have a working knowledge of the technology their company relies on and how it will improve their business. Comprehension of their technology systems allows them to make quality technology-based decisions when issues arise.

- Agile decision-making skills – The reality of VUCA is that CEOs must be quick to act decisively when a situation develops. While some would say it's better to make a wrong decision than no decision, it is easier said than done when the stakes are high. In general, CEOs battle the idea of making too many mistakes, but the answer is not to avoid the error but to improve their decision-making skills to make smart decisions quickly. Without learning agility, leaders will be less prepared for an uncertain future and be more likely to repeat past mistakes.

- The power to inspire – CEOs are always under the gun. They are inspired by the vision they set, and it's what often gets them through the mounting demands of the job. Being a CEO is not for the faint of heart. In my experience and that of my clients, few people truly understand what that's like. Still, it is not enough for them to be inspired. It is essential to inspire those around you, your teams, and the public with a compelling vision of hope and success for the company. Doing so will diametrically affect the company's bottom line.

- The ability to assemble a great team – We've gone from companies saying, 'Our people are our greatest asset' and showing it to companies that say it and don't show it. The best talent wants to work for a company they can trust and admire. Exceptional leaders will attract the most outstanding talent. Becoming an exceptional leader must be a conscious decision, not just a slogan or tagline you hang in your office. Good intentions don't mean a thing. Exceptional leaders know how to lead by knowing themselves first and then knowing their team to know what they need and from whom.

Whether you are a professional, current or aspiring leader or CEO, the right combination of these skills will give you a competitive edge. As a business and brain science coach, I continually track the trends that cause the most disruption to humans with future readiness in mind, hence my Human-First Performance Systems™. One example is Deloitte Insights, which discusses the concept of the 'No-Collar Workforce.'[46] The term, no-collar workforce, pertains to the drive to create a powerful collaboration of humans and technology where the unique strengths of both can be leveraged to achieve intelligent automation.

---

46 https://www2.deloitte.com/us/en/insights/focus/tech-trends/2018/no-collar-workforce.html

Essentially, it evaluates humans and machines in one loop as a combined unit.

Technological advances have already set the premise that technology reaches beyond automating labor jobs. Many companies have developed expertise automation AI-based solutions for white-collar jobs. White-collar jobs impacted by these technologies include lawyers, HR managers, marketers, teaching assistants, reporters and editors, traders, accountants and auditors, compliance officers, and investment managers, to name a few.

To become future-ready, you must understand your role in working alongside machines and the unique value you bring to the table. Billions of dollars are invested each year in this type of automation. Machines are not going away as they will serve a strong purpose in augmenting humans' work. Work environments are evaluated to achieve the best combination of humans and machines across two dimensions: abilities and skills.

Abilities include psychomotor, sensory, physical, and cognitive. Skills include content, process, system, and social. Humans' only advantages over machines come down to cognitive abilities and social skills. Unfortunately, these have been steadily declining in focus and development over the last two decades. Companies stopped investing in the development of their employees through priority shifting and commoditization of talent driven by cost-cutting and maximizing output.

Many jobs have already gone away because of disruptive technology and automation. We've gone from brick and mortar to click and order, from butts in the seat to eyes on the screen. These disruptions have been thrust upon us, forever changing life and the economy. We are now in a learning-based, not knowledge-based, economy. Yes, many jobs will go away, but new jobs are also being created that require the skills I mentioned above.

The great thing about innovation

Despite this chapter's title, there are enormous upsides to innovation. Too many to cover here, but I'll mention a few. Were it not for innovation-driven thinkers, we would not see today's incredible advances and game-changing technologies that have improved our lives and our world. Take, for example, Bioprinting. As technology improves, corporates are exploring opportunities to print organs for regenerative medicine applications that enable the creation of living biological tissue and printing entire organ-like kidneys and lungs without the risk of rejection and waiting for a donor match.

Other healthcare sector game-changers include space-based research and development and Ambient Intelligence to improve bedside care at clinics, hospitals, and assisted living facilities, given the growth of the aging population.

Another sector is the environment. For example, the emission crisis is being mitigated by green hydrogen – a true zero-emission source of power aimed at the high emission, power-consuming industries like transportation and heavy industry.

Game-changer tech companies want to transform society and economies as they disrupt almost every sector and industry. It is fun and exciting being a disruptor with a good cause. Of course, the underlying technologies are a combination of AI, Machine Learning, Deep Learning, Blockchain, robotics, nanotechnology, and others. The flip side is that this also opens a lot of new and more sophisticated threats like cybersecurity issues, exploitative fraud, and many more.

As I mentioned earlier, the 21st century is a time of greatly accelerated scientific discovery. Cars are driving themselves. Vaccines against deadly new viruses are created in less than a year instead of the previously typical 15 years and $15B of investment required to get a drug to market. Private space travel has been proven possible while the latest Mars Rover is hunting for signs of alien life.

The fly in the soup? We're also surrounded by outdated scientific myths and mental models that regularly make their way into news stories and social media, creating confusion and misinformation. I experienced this with nanotechnology private social media watchdogs with baseless claims that compared it to asbestos. Need I remind you of the Genetically Modified Organism or GMO safety debacle? Tragically, Monsanto made bad judgment decisions on how to manage and 'protect' their IP, but that does not mean the GMO-enhanced food was dangerous 'frankenfood.' Our farming ancestors had done selective breeding and crossbreeding for centuries. It would be good to consider that today's tasty apples did not exist in those early days. The main point here is that people have higher difficulties discerning what's accurate and what is not.

New avenues for crime

But let's get back to more current times. In March 2021, the Federal Bureau of Investigation (FBI) declared that technologies such as audio and video-based deepfakes are already here and not something of the future. Of course, they'd been out years prior, but now it allowed malicious actors to go after higher and higher stakes. You may have heard of many hacking incidents, like the imitated voice of a CEO used to initiate a wire transfer of $243K created by or altered by AI or machine learning.

Or the theft of $600M worth of cryptocurrency from PolyNetworks, a platform connecting several blockchains. The cybercriminals returned most of the funds. However, we can see a clear example of the type of Pandora's Box we are opening for society with sophisticated yet unregulated technologies.

For decades, I've observed the rate of new and more sophisticated technologies used in phishing and other scam tactics on unsuspecting victims. I study and analyze the perpetrators' behavioral patterns and the victims' vulnerability factors in my research. I also saw how these scams increased during the height of the pandemic lockdowns in 2020. Objectively speaking, the cons are brilliantly executed and leverage the effects of VUCA to their advantage.

Many of these enabling technologies have already debuted in mainstream markets. Unfortunately, people have been training their brains to make decisions not based on systems thinking and emotional intelligence, thus creating vulnerabilities that malicious actors can exploit.

So, if you're wondering how the F* can we navigate through the noise and make smarter decisions, here are some things you can start doing.

a. Stop and smell the metaphorical innovation roses. Start by asking yourself, what does that mean for me and others? For my job/profession? For my industry? For my family or my kids' future?

b. Question everything but do it with an open and learning mind instead of being driven by irrelevant mental models that lead you astray or allowing your biases to get in the way of learning.

c. Know yourself and discover your blind spots because avoiding them is essential to managing smart decision-making processes.

d. Understand that, more often than not, we fall into a hamster wheel of doing whatever it takes in the name of perceived efficiency. That means avoid looking for a magic pill, a quick fix, or a less-than-well-thought-out innovation launched to the masses before it is fully baked.

e. Become more aware of whether you are actually making a decision or just going along with groupthink and the opinions of others who already think exactly like you do. If they think like you and your decision-making track record has not been great, run the other way.

f. Develop the courage to actively seek the opinion of those who do not think like you to challenge your assumptions. It is a necessary practice for growth as long as you don't forget b and c above. At the same time, remember that the world is paved with good intentions to solve societal problems, and everyone thinks they have the better mousetrap.

g. Remember, you can't possibly know what you want until you know who you are (Chapter 1)—and knowing yourself also includes examining your values. Ask yourself, is this decision in alignment with my values? Support your values and protect your soul.

h. Despite good intentions, we may inevitably encounter some unintended consequences. So, keep a watchful eye and pay attention to what is happening around you. It is another great opportunity to grow from lessons learned.

i. Use systems thinking to allow you to detect, mitigate, and even thrive in VUCA. Yes, it is possible to thrive when you master it. If you can train yourself to avoid using inflexible, autocratic management styles, you'll be able to make smarter, quicker, more balanced decisions.

These and other techniques are what I use to spot trends and behavior shifts that allow me to be prepared and minimize or eliminate the impact of threats and disruptions. It served me in my career trajectories from continual learning to contrarian investing to nanotechnologies to being prepared and avoiding the effects of the pandemic.

You could argue that perhaps luck was on my side. The truth is that the more prepared I was, the luckier I got. That's why I've never allowed myself to rely on chance. What's certain is that I was very intentional in my decisions, and when I made a wrong decision, I dissected it to learn from the misstep. I also had a clear vision of what I wanted and problem-solved my way to achieving it.

Today I incorporate the systems and skills I've honed over three decades into my Human-First Performance Systems™, combining systems-thinking techniques and mindsets with adaptability and emotional intelligence. I've learned that this is the only way to become resilient and future-ready. It's the only way you can adapt, improvise, and overcome. I love to help others conquer challenges, face fear, build confidence, and thrive in VUCA. It is the reason I am writing this book.

The danger of cognitive bias in AI

Earlier, I discussed the trends in AI and the promises and challenges that come with it. Have you ever felt frustrated when a machine learning algorithm made the wrong decision, and you could not clarify it? For example, I recall when major credit card companies started using AI to detect fraud. You would think that is a good thing, except that it was primarily for the benefit of the credit card company, not the cardholder. I say this because it was so quick to block the transaction but did nothing to automate communication with the cardholder and verify the purchase in real time. I was told that a flag was placed on my account, and a letter was initiated to be mailed to the account holder's billing address. And that's supposed to help me how?

It burdens the cardholder to sit through painful automated phone systems to find a real person to talk to, further adding to the frustration. I must say it has improved over the last eight years or so. Even recently, however, my husband was at our vacation property to finish some home improvement projects. He was blocked from purchasing items at Home Depot. He called me because I'm the master account holder and wanted to know if I had been notified of a flag. I had not. He was in a hurry, so he used a different credit card. Three hours later, I received a text from the bank asking if we had tried to make a purchase at Home Depot and gave the amount. I replied 'yes' to clear the flag. It answered back, saying that we could resume the transaction and that it would go through. Did the AI think my husband would still be standing at the Home Depot waiting to make his purchase three hours later?

Here's the problem: mistakes in neural networks are more common than you think. This happens for two main reasons: First, they are developed by naturally biased humans who likely do not possess enough emotional intelligence to aid in their decision-making processes. Second, they don't set adequate boundaries and parameters to avoid the technology's downsides. This could also be for the same reason related to EQ. AI-based technologies cannot apply human reasoning to data and only depend on the most straightforward interpretations. This means your result would be very quick but could also be very wrong. The human brain is better at processing information that is not straightforward. Yet very few things are straightforward anymore, hence VUCA. This leads to a vicious loop that gets faster and increasingly feeds bad information to a company's business processes that can negatively affect it in the long term.

Companies (and their leaders) must understand how the technology works and ensure that the system has implemented bias-reduction measures that work. Unlike humans, artificial intelligence has difficulty overcoming biases to reach optimal business outcomes. AI systems don't have opinions; instead, they receive input and information from biased human perspectives. Leaders should not rely on algorithms alone to make and execute all decisions as business decisions. A solid bias-aware human element – called Human in the Loop – should be involved in evaluating the quality of information if something goes wrong. It is worth repeating that humans need to be trained and deeply understand their own behaviors, biases, driving forces, and emotional intelligence to evaluate the quality of the information from an AI system and apply human reasoning. The stakes are high when you are too inexperienced, nervous, rattled, or vulnerable to make decisions during a crisis.

Today, businesses have to make trade-offs between accuracy and efficiency. The trade-off builds the case for making AI algorithms think more like humans in the future. Trying to evaluate a solution that provides more nuanced results and relies solely on how AI thinks someone will answer in a particular situation will be even more complex.

So, where do you go from here? The bottom line is that the future is not just about automating and improving processes; it's about decisions and tasks that, up to now, typically humans did. So, is it better to improve AI systems or humans? Keeping in mind that improvement means doing what's difficult, humans must learn to overcome their biases before machines overcome their limitations.

Key takeaways

- Innovation holds tremendous promise to continue improving our lives, but there is a dark side where no regulation exists, and consumers are the testing ground. We need to proceed with eyes wide open. Consumers are becoming addicted and want more but remember caveat emptor – the buyer alone is responsible for checking the quality and sustainability of goods before the purchase.
- Our behaviors, motivators, and decision-making progress are tied directly to skill development. Watch out for scams.
- We make emotional decisions. Build your EQ and turn your emotions into your superpower, not your secret kryptonite.
- Biases and blind spots are the enemies of smart decision-making. Discover them and factor them into your decision-making process.
- Cognitive bias baked into AI systems can harm businesses.

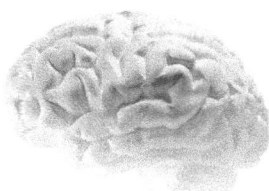

CHAPTER 7

FAILURE IS YOUR FRIEND

You are not failing. You are growing.

If you dread the idea of failing, take comfort, for the world is full of failures, and you are in good company.

Failure is how our ancestors survived. Failure is how we learn to walk, sit, eat, read, play sports, create music, invent, create wealth, and push ideas that become movements. In my previous book, *11 Ways To Improve Your Human Condition*, I mention how people like Michael Jordan, Warren Buffet, Richard Branson, and Jack Ma failed. Here are a few other famous failures:

- Oprah Winfrey was told she'd never make it on television and was fired from her first television job as an anchor for getting too emotionally invested in her stories. She is now a multi-billionaire and one of the most influential women globally.

- Steve Jobs was fired from Apple, a company he co-founded, at age 30. However, he returned to Apple years later and played a key role in launching game-changing products like the iPod, iPad, and iPhone.

- Walt Disney was fired from the Kansas City Star because he "lacked imagination and had no good ideas," according to his editor. The Walt Disney Company is now one of the largest and best-known studios in Hollywood.

- Bill Gates dropped out of Harvard and co-founded a failed first business, Traf-O-Data. Despite these early setbacks, he co-founded Microsoft and is now one of the wealthiest individuals in the world.

How I failed my way to tremendous success

Allow me to share a few of the many *What was I thinking?* moments that proved pivotal in shaping my life. These moments earned their name as my surprised conscious brain made me ask, *"What was I thinking?"* I discovered later that my actions were driven by my subconscious overwriting what my conscious brain was telling me. You might even think of them as epiphanies heard only when I listened to them instead of succumbing to outside noises.

I knew I had something in me that started to surface at age seven. I did not know it then, but it was the power of desire—for me, it was to have a better life than my mom had had. Therefore, I rebelled, *a lot,* and deliberately went against my mom's teachings and commands, questioning everything. Imagine her joy!

It wasn't until the ripe age of 18 that I learned its meaning. *"Your burning desire is nothing more than an accurate picture of what you will one day become."* Remember, I had no role models. I had to figure things out for myself. I'd take every opportunity to learn from people outside my family who were professionals. This power of desire drove me to enter the workforce at age 14, graduate high school at 16, get married at 16, and get divorced at 18. Despite what it might look like, none of these were failures. Why? After he hit me a couple of times, it was apparent he was not my way to a better life. I refused to be a victim like my mom and would be better off without him.

Failure comes from not learning the lesson and not taking positive action. Success comes from lessons learned in failure and taking the right action.

I would continue on my path to achieving the life I wanted and deserved. My burning desire kept me focused on the goal but with a mind open to alternative ways of getting there, new mental models, and a hunger to learn. Here are a few *What was I thinking?* adventures that required risk with a high possibility of failure.

1. What was I thinking? Leave Laredo alone? I was taking charge of my life and making my own destiny.

   a. In a small town, you get a lot of crab syndrome, which you must learn to navigate. You have to fight them off to get out or let them keep you in the bucket with them. Keeping your eyes on the ball is everything.

   b. By age 20, I had dropped out of community college because I had a business idea inspired by a story I read in the *Entrepreneur* magazine I picked up at a friend's hair salon. I didn't know what an entrepreneur was, but the magazine caught my attention and sparked a business vision.

   c. The Business: the first software retail store in Texas. I chose San Antonio because it was a better market. I spent many months researching a location and writing a business plan to secure a Small Business Administration (SBA) loan. It would require a $20K personal injection, which I did not have, so I recruited a silent investor.

   d. When the time came to ante up, my silent investor backed out – he wanted a piece of me, not just a part of the business. I would not sell myself like that, so I walked away heartbroken but with my integrity and self-respect intact.

e. I was four years ahead of the very successful EggHead Software franchise chain founded in 1984. That would've been a nice exit.

Biggest reward: I gained valuable lessons through the **power of persistence**. I moved back to Laredo and got back on my feet with a great job and good pay. I was learning to play golf, training in martial arts, and competing successfully in tournaments all over Texas. All was seemingly good.

And then…it hit me.

2. What was I thinking? Go back to school but now at the University of Texas, Austin?

a. It meant being a 'poor student' again – no big car, decent salary, etc.

b. It meant being in classrooms of 300 students and a competitive program.

c. I was the first person in my family to apply and be accepted to a major university – with no role models showing me the way.

d. It would mean graduating ten years after high school – no classmates, but that was unimportant because I was on a mission.

e. I'd have to figure out how to do this financially while still helping to support my mom. I competed for loans and grants, plus secured two part-time jobs while carrying a full course load.

f. While there, my subconscious went to work – One day, I randomly veered off my path to cut through the Electrical Engineering (EE) building. I had no classes there, but I was curious. I noticed a sheet on a door window with assigned interview times with an HP manager representing the database labs. I had no appointment and was not an EE student, so I waited until the manager came out and told her I'd just noticed this and while I wasn't an EE student, I was familiar with HP servers as a programmer in a previous job. The manager liked my initiative and opened a spot for the next day. My trajectory would've been different if I had not taken this risk and detour.

<u>Biggest Rewards:</u>

- It led me to an internship program at Hewlett Packard in the heart of Silicon Valley, California.
- Working with super smart professional people from different parts of the world.
- Getting excellent professional growth training.
- Adopting DWSYWD (<u>d</u>o <u>w</u>hat <u>y</u>ou <u>s</u>ay <u>y</u>ou <u>w</u>ill <u>d</u>o) as one of the tenets after learning it from HP CEO Lew Platt.

3. What was I thinking? Date the Geek?

    a. There were tons of promising prospects on the fast track at HP and in the Bay Area in general.

    b. But, without consciously intending to and against my friend's advice, I dated the geek.

        i. He was cute but not stylish and drove an old beat-up Ford Falcon. My friend told me I could do much better than that.

        ii. He did not show big career ambition and was younger than me. I was career-ambitious and more experienced.

        iii. I had no interest in settling down – I was too independent.

        iv. Work colleagues were shocked when they learned we had become an item because I was a rampant independent woman, and he was an unassuming, polite engineer.

<u>Biggest Reward:</u> For the last 31 years and counting, I continue to feel grateful for allowing him into my life as we created the most fabulous, loving family. Once again, my subconscious knew better. More on this later.

4. What was I thinking? Leaving the high-tech industry?

    a. High-tech imploded in 2001 with the dot.com bubble, and thousands lost their jobs.

b. In the spirit of the book *"Who Moved My Cheese"* by Spencer Johnson, MD, I opened my mind to other possibilities.

c. My reframe: I didn't lose a job, I gained an opportunity to research and explore several business ideas. To find 'new cheese.'

d. After all, with my life experience, I also knew that: *"Life is not about waiting for the storm to pass, it's about learning to dance in the rain."* – Vivian Green

e. I also fervently believe that only those who risk going too far can possibly find out how far they can go. I had come far, but I was not done.

<u>Biggest Reward:</u> It allowed me to explore and rediscover my passions and dive back into the entrepreneurial world.

a. I embarked on a journey to the biotech and nanotech industries – I was tracking tech trends and loved science.

b. I built a business that was hugely successful in the nanotechnology arena.

c. I established credibility among PhDs, MD/PhDs, entrepreneurs, government agencies, and research universities and institutes.

After years of studying and analysis, I discovered the answer to the 'What was I thinking?' questions above: *I was not thinking*! Each of those times, I ignored my conscious mind, which is too often tainted by misguided biases and beliefs, and instead followed my subconscious and intuition; my burning desire was to have a better life and break the cycle of poverty, and my subconscious was working on it, guiding me throughout. I succeeded despite myself, despite my conscious (at the time) rigid beliefs that sometimes set me back a bit, but I learned valuable lessons each time.

If you think this is all about discipline and willpower, think again. Will and discipline might help you do more repetitions at the gym or skip the slice of cake, but that won't do it for your subconscious. You can't just flip on a switch and turn your subconscious on because it is always on. Not only that, but it is also always listening to you. You have to hone it with practice, genuine reflection, a learning mind, and the tools and techniques I've developed to make your brain work for you and not against you.

Beyond observations and research, I accepted the notion that I'd be in good company by admiring people who struggled and persevered versus those who had little to no struggles in getting to where they were. It meant achieving despite the lack of privilege. All the setbacks and mistakes throughout are what I've learned to call the **fertilizer of failure,** a term I picked up from actor Ryan Reynolds in an interview about his entrepreneurial ventures and his learned lessons. Even with his fame and clout, he has failed in a few ventures but keeps learning and applying those lessons in each new iteration. If you are learning and taking action, you get better each time. This is why failing is a gift.

I see the fertilizer of failure as what a person needs the most to enrich the soil from which the best stuff can grow - confidence, wisdom, discovery, bravery, courage, and enjoyment.

Yet millions of people worldwide hold themselves back because they are afraid to fail. This behavior pattern has fascinated me because it has a lot to do with how the brain works, how we make decisions, how we handle adversity, and how we become resilient. I set out to decode the links in similar ways as I would debug software to find the faulty instruction code. The pathways are many because there are infinite combinations of factors involved, experiences, and patterns woven into the person you have become. It's what makes us all unique, and at the same time, we all can be suggestible and fall into traps of our own making, which negates the concept of failure as a positive. Infused with biases against taking risks, your brain nudges you to play it safe instead. However, taking the safe route is not safe at all.

How we make decisions

The average person is estimated to make 35,000 decisions daily, or about 2,000 per hour or one every two seconds.

Unbelievable, right? Researchers at Cornell University found that we make 226.7 daily decisions on food alone.[47]

Different styles and inclinations influence how you make decisions. Your decisions could be driven by impulsiveness, compliance, delegating, avoidance/deflection, balancing, prioritizing, or reflecting. These driving forces often combine to factor in the decision-making process depending on the situation and the volume of decisions you have to make.

As I've mentioned a few times throughout this book, the fact remains that when there are options, we are not a product of our circumstances - we are a product of our decisions. People often find themselves in a rut, but those ruts don't dig themselves. Allowing yourself to be a product of circumstances places the burden of responsibility for how your life turns out on someone else. When you had options but chose poorly, this victim mentality also removes accountability and responsibility, destroying your confidence and impairing your mental health. The outcomes result from your actions, actions that become habits and, by definition, are repeated because they feel safe only through familiarity.

The easiest way to stop making bad choices is to stop making bad choices. How? Start by identifying the

---

47   Wansink, B. & Sobal, J. (2007). Mindless eating. The 200 daily
        food decisions we overlook. Environment and Behaviour, 39, 106-
        123.

triggers that lead you to bad decisions and remove those triggers. Tiny changes help break bad habits and create new ones.

Another point I've previously taught is that there is no such thing as making a truly rational decision because an emotion is always tied to it somewhere deep down. Emotions are a natural and significant part of your decision-making process. You can deny that you make emotional decisions until you are blue in the face. Still, your brain simply ignores how strategic, rational, objective, or analytical you so proudly think you are.[48]

This concept can ruffle the feathers of the stern executives and some members of the analytical or scientific communities I've worked with. Each time it comes up, they will push back as they deny this is the case. Part of the debate is the belief that rational decisions are the best decisions, but all it is a well-seated bias and blind spot when it is not recognized or accepted.

Science speaks out: In the argument of whether the best decisions are rational or emotional, the scientific jury is in - **emotions win**.

A current peer-reviewed research paper supports this position and affirms that skills are experience-based and tied to emotional reactions. The "Brain Activation

48   https://www.linkedin.com/pulse/woulda-coulda-shoulda-dilem-ma-adriana-vela-1c/

Imaging in Emotional Decision-Making and Mental Health" report by Thomas F. Collura, Ph.D. and Ronald J Bonnstetter, Ph.D., was submitted to the Clinical EEG and Neuroscience journal. [49]

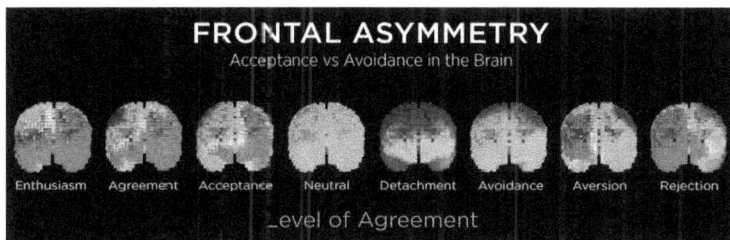

Image courtesy of Ronald J Bonnstetter, Ph.D., Director of the TTI Center for Applied Cognitive Research

The report demonstrates an operational model for emotional decision-making that incorporates brain activation data and subjective experience correlations. The model functions like a state machine that handles transitions between a finite set of sixteen possible states of emotional and decision-making responses. EEG technology that produces a millisecond-resolution representation of the brain activity corroborates a direct reflection of emotional processing and, hence, that decisions are based firmly on emotions. These findings may be perceived as a threat to traditional mindsets.

49   Bonnstetter, Ronald & Collura, Thomas. (2020). Brain Activation Imaging in Emotional Decision Making and Mental Health: A Review—Part 1. Clinical EEG and Neuroscience. 52. 155005942091663. 10.1177/1550059420916636.

Turn a threat into an opportunity

We must first acknowledge that all decisions are emotional.

Key point: You can use this as your superpower instead of thinking of it as your kryptonite. What is this power called? It's called Emotional Intelligence and measured as Emotional Quotient or EQ.

Raising your EQ is essential here because making better decisions requires tools that help you assess background information systematically. Here's why: Emotional intelligence will make you more apt to surround yourself with people who will challenge your opinions. You'll be able to empathetically listen as they tell you things you may not want to hear but must. This is the essence of personal growth.

If you do, you can turn it to your advantage by tapping into it. Just don't tap too hard – recall the concept of *self-regulation.*

Why is it hard to make rational decisions? Humans fail to make rational decisions in the decision-making process when assessing risk because our brains take mental shortcuts. These shortcuts, also called heuristics, allow people to solve problems and make judgments quickly and efficiently. It's a rule of thumb or educated guess, possibly based on an established pattern already embedded in your thinking or silently trapped emotions, biases, and blind spots. Using this as a decision-making strategy prevents us from making the correct decision that will serve us best.

Over the years, I've curated dozens of top-notch decision-making models because there is no one-size-fits-all. My philosophy:

Not all problems are nails and, therefore, not all solutions should be hammers.

The key is to take the first step, get past denying, and exercise a balanced judgment. Next, you also want to ensure your psychological biases are in check. Only then can you move forward and address the most critical issues in your decision-making processes - psychological biases, also known as *cognitive biases.* Cognitive biases impact how we interpret, judge, and remember information. It is good to note that not all biases are negative, as they are a hard-wired part of our cognition and decision-making.

Everyone is susceptible to psychological bias, a concept introduced in the early 1970s by psychologists Daniel Kahneman, Paul Slovic, and Amos Tversky. It is worth noting that behavioral and cognitive scientists, neuroscientists, and psychologists have identified over 175 cognitive biases, and the research continues. Here are a few that can cause havoc when assessing risk in business.

We should be aware of their existence because they can lead to missed opportunities and poor decisions. Here are a select few I highly recommend you learn about and avoid.

- Confirmation Bias – Focusing only on information that confirms existing preconceptions. Relying on it is not helpful when you need to change course because the world is changing rapidly. 'We did loads of simulations. Most of them showed there's no problem.' The key is to be proactive in seeking objectivity.
- Anchoring effect – Relying too much on the initial piece of information offered when making a decision. 'The first test seemed ok. Do we need to look any more?'
- Bandwagon Effect – The uptake of beliefs and ideas increases the more that others have already adopted them. 'The whole department knows there's no problem here.' It is strongly related to groupthink and herd mentality.
- Gambler's Fallacy – Believing that future probabilities are altered by past events when they are unchanged. 'The conveyor belt broke three times last month. It's pretty unlikely it'll happen again.'
- Overconfidence Bias or Illusion of Validity – when a person tends to overestimate their ability to make accurate predictions, especially when data appears to tell a coherent "story." 'This worked fine in the factory in Korea, so it should work fine here.'

"You can fail at what you don't like doing, so might as well fail at doing what you love." –Jim Carrey

Research has consistently shown that we are often better off when we fail. Why? Because when we fail, we grow, build resiliency, use more creativity, and become great problem solvers. We also become problem finders, which means we get better at detecting, anticipating, and making smarter decisions. Own the failures as much as you own the wins. It may sound esoteric, but it changes *everything*. If you take a fresh perspective on failures and open your mind to the valuable lessons you gain, owning your failure becomes a badge of honor. Wearing it proudly for honor and integrity fuels your self-esteem and feeds your soul. I've learned and witnessed this for decades.

You can be the sweetest peach in the world, but there will always be some people who don't like peaches.

Common reasons people avoid the possibility of failure – sometimes at all costs

To be clear, I'm not asking you to *like* failure. It is perfectly human to dislike it. If I were, I'd be asking you to go against existing mental models, and we know how that worked out for Dr. Semmelweis in Chapter 6, don't we? Instead, this section is about empowering you to explore a different mental model that will build your confidence and allow you to experience more success than you ever imagined.

The first step is to consider these top 10 unexamined possible reasons that hold you back from taking action toward your goals and dreams. Perhaps it's time for one of my pieces of training called a Mindset Reset, seeing failure more as a friend than a foe. Which one of these feels familiar to you? Fair warning: what follows directly tells it like it is because I care about you too much to let you stay the same.

1. **What if you don't really want to succeed?**

   a. Are you challenging your own internal status quo in decision-making?
   b. Are you in a comfort addiction trap? It's easy to stay comfortable with things you know; you build fictitious trust only because it is familiar.
   c. Are you self-sabotaging? Perhaps setting yourself unconscious traps that keep you in that comfort zone?
   d. Are you really valuing the privileges you have?
   e. Are your goals aligned with your values?
   f. Have you discovered your hidden talents?

2. **You worry about what may never happen, which only creates an illusion of control.**

   a. Worry is the most useless emotion because it spends your body's resources on something that may never happen! Worry gives you an illusion that you have control when you have no control.

b. You worry that you need luck fueled by the 'I always have bad luck' mindset. 'I never get what I want' instead of making do with what you have. You justify your worry or pessimism to yourself to maintain the illusion. Be resourceful instead! MacGyver the shit out of things.

3. Have a lousy perspective on failure.

a. This means that you have a lousy self-identity with a strong hold on you: *"If I fail at this, I'm a failure."* You believe that the outcomes reflect who you are as a person. It's not about failure but what you learn from failure. That's why comeback stories are inspiring - you can come back from setbacks, but you need to change your perspective on failure. As sure as death and taxes, there will be failures and disruptions. Some might be of your own making, but you can come back from that.

b. It is hard to let go of a deep-seated perspective or bias because there is a tendency to somehow find comfort in what we are familiar with rather than the unfamiliar. Ever heard the saying, *"Better the devil we know than the one we don't"*? This is just a fallacy to keep you where you are. It stems from fear of the unknown and the psychological principle known as "loss aversion," where people strongly prefer avoiding losses over acquiring gains.

c. It is harder to unlearn something than to learn something new. The brain will default to bad habits instead of new ones because of the previously established patterns. New situations have your brain busy trying to make meaning out of them, which means it cannot spend energy on making smart decisions unless you already have those patterns built. Your brain will look for the easy way out. Not because it is lazy but because it is doing body budgeting, which is why it defaults back to old habits. When the situation is uncertain, uncertainty becomes the seed for anxiety, and anxiety fuels fear. New habits takes time and practice- you can't will yourself to do them. Many baby steps really do add up! You must build your brain up over time. You go from conscious incompetent to unconscious competent, like when you learned to drive.

d. You can't distinguish between a bad risk and a smart risk. System's thinking and lateral thinking are the techniques that help with this distinction. Mastering these skills will improve your life on so many levels.

e. How we look at things determines whether something is good or bad. *"Men are disturbed not by the things that happen, but by their opinion of the things that happen."* — Epictetus

4. **We fool ourselves about what we need to take action (control, perfectionism, etc.).**

a. I learned that you need to start taking 'imperfect actions.' You've been doing this all along when you learned something for the first time—riding a bike, driving, cooking, doing taxes (ugh), interviewing for your first job. Be brave enough to suck at something new! You get better at it with practice.

b. The problem with control is that we often want to control those things we have no control over. In some, it could be triggered by worry and the illusory need to feel like we have control or by the fear of letting go and being okay with it.

c. Avoid the perfectionist paradox (something I often battle with and am mindful to keep in check).

5. **We think we know ourselves, but we really don't.**

a. **Socrates:** *"An unexamined life is not worth living."* The Stoics borrowed this idea from Socrates because they emphasized the ability to admit our weaknesses and fallibility by reflecting on and criticizing our own character. This is to be done honestly and constructively for the purpose of continually improving ourselves. In the context of failure, this means being ok with failing because it is all about self-improvement.

b. Some people only exist. They don't live. Their eyes are open, but they are asleep at the wheel of their own vehicle, taking them who knows where. Wake up, smell reality, and take control of where you want to go.

c. Are you making snap decisions solely based on confirmation bias or your value judgments? What if you are wrong about them? What if your previous failures do *not* represent a guarantee that you'll fail again? Clearly, if you are doing the same thing repeatedly and expecting different results, that's just the definition of insanity! But that's not what I'm talking about here. I'm talking about trying or exploring something new that gets you out of your comfort zone and expands your reach to achieve the life you've always wanted.

6. **We have misaligned or outright delusional expectations.**

a. Like the armchair quarterback who believes he could do a better job. They don't put in the work- they're not out there, and if you tell them this is what it would take for them to do that better job, they'd probably chicken out.

b. Or the confusion between having a passion and having an ability. I have a passion for dancing, but I know I would not stand a chance to compete in the TV show "So You Think You Can Dance." You must be realistic about your abilities.

c. Thinking you'll never bounce back from this failure. This type of thinking is often tied to maladaptive behaviors, cognitive distortions, or avoidant personalities that often lead to self-sabotage or burnout. The failure is not the culprit; the action or behavior is.

d. You feel that your life/career/relationship/ will be over. Nobody ever died from trying something new unless it was jumping out of a perfectly good airplane without their parachute. Putting the drama aside, this misalignment could be based on equating success with 'not failing.'

    i. This is the time to change your perspective on what success is. Most people define success as possible only through rigid discipline, methodologies, or mindsets. That is not what success is. Success comes down to learning and growing. It is fuel for the soul, the experience of pursuing a challenge or hurdle, and not the actual outcome.

ii. Here's the proof: Are you not successful if you learned powerful lessons that will help you in the next iteration or the rest of your future? Or to have become wiser and achieved an expanded mind you can harvest for many more opportunities that come your way? Is it not a success to learn to become adaptable when new challenges are thrust upon you, whether you want them or not? As Bruce Lee puts it, being water *is* success. *"Don't get set into one form, adapt it, and build your own, and let it grow, be like water. Empty your mind, be formless, shapeless — like water. Now, you put water in a cup, it becomes the cup; you put water into a bottle, it becomes the bottle; you put it in a teapot, it becomes the teapot. Now water can flow, or it can crash. Be water, my friend."* — Bruce Lee

7. **We take or follow the wrong advice (outdated teachings). Which have you heard the most?**

a. "If you don't gamble, you won't lose." – Yes, that statement is factual; however, if you don't gamble, your only guarantee is that you won't win either.

b. "Never give up" intends to motivate you to stick to a practice or approach unsuitable for you. Whether it is a weight loss plan, a workout plan, a career plan, or another, you need to be willing to face what the world is telling you, what your body is telling you, and what your developed systems thinking is telling you. For example, if you find yourself in a cul-de-sac and can't find the address, do you continue going round and round, or do you quit the effort and try something new? Learn to identify that pattern and quit the cul-de-sac.

c. "Follow your passion" – Think about it. Is it really possible to only have one passion? Should we follow all of them? What if we are passionate about the idea of something, but it would never work or make us happy?

d. "Live each day as if it were your last." Stop and think about this one. If this was really your last day, would you want to spend it doing good work, self-development, eating healthy, etc? Work on things that will help you prepare for tomorrow? Instead, you'd be happier living each day grateful and celebrating what you have.

e. "Failure is not an option" – Nothing could be further from the truth. Failure is not something you take or leave; it is a reality of life. It happens to EVERYONE, ANYTIME, ANYPLACE, ANYWHERE! Let me define failure for you in one word: NECESSARY. Yes, it is, and I'll prove it to you!

i. We are born failures – we can't feed ourselves, we can't walk, communicate, and keep ourselves warm. But we learn, don't we? Little by little and with help and practice, we get better and better until we become self-sufficient. We don't just come off the street and pass a driving test without ever getting behind the wheel, do we? You don't ride a bike perfectly the first time you hop on the seat.

ii. If you are a start-up preparing a Hail Mary pitch to get funding for your company, you've heard this phrase in your head or from someone else. Or perhaps when you're working on a critical proposal, the completion and acceptance of which would mean getting the client or losing to the competition, you've heard this phrase. The phrase "failure is not an option" may not be an option you would seek, but it will always be possible.

8. We don't have faith (Jim Carrey – faith, not religion)

a. Actor Jim Carrey gave the commencement speech for MUM University in 2014. Before I watched it, I was eager because I thought it would be entertaining. It did not disappoint in that area, but I was not expecting the profound perspective he shared as he told the story about his father, who worked hard at a company doing what he did not enjoy to provide for the family. Like many of us who are responsible and accountability-minded, we do what we have to do, and hopefully, later, we can do what we want to do. Jim reflected on how grateful he was to be able to do what he loved and that people he met presented their best selves to him. Then, he shared his transformational message. *"Take a chance on faith. Not religion, faith. Not hope, faith. I don't believe in hope. Hope is a beggar. Hope walks through the fire, but faith leaps over it!"*

There have been many fires that I leaped over because I knew that if I didn't, nothing would change. Without faith in myself, I would not have been able to break the chains of poverty and live a life without physical or emotional abuse. Taking risks and risking failure led me instead to a life filled with support and encouragement, trust, love, gratitude, and appreciat on. I live comfortably and have a beautiful, loving family. A life that I could only dream of when I was growing up.

b. You are possibly giving in to imposter syndrome. This affliction is experienced by every human being multiple times in their lives. It is a dysfunctional way of thinking that allows fear to hold you back from taking forward action. It is often rooted in shame, and the sheer thought of being discovered or called out as an imposter is unbearable (remember, I spoke about the emotion of shame as a type of social pain in Chapter 4). The reframe is to recognize that the total absence of imposter syndrome means you are not growing and expanding. Start getting comfortable with being uncomfortable for a bit. When that feeling is completely gone again, it will be time to look for the next opportunity to experience imposter syndrome and keep growing.

c. Steer clear of people who, when "bad things" inevitably happen, their world collapses, and they panic inconsolably. A leader does not have the luxury of panicking, nor do they want it, because when things go south, their first instinct is to problem-solve, minimize impact, and come up with a solution. Lastly, they learn from it. If this is you, congratulations. If not, it is okay, but you must develop this to lead yourself and others successfully

9. **Strangely, however, I see people often placing too much faith in the opinions of others.**

    a. Opinions. Everybody has them. Inevitably, you'll come across others who might think less of you.

    b. Start by questioning who these 'others' are and if they are worth your concern. More often than not, they either don't know you, won't notice, or care, as they are probably worrying about themselves and trying to look good.

    c. You'll be criticized or judged no matter what, so let it go. Get used to the fact that being judged is human nature. Sounds simple, but it is not, and why I covered it in Chapter 4 regarding social pain.

    d. Are you giving up what you want to satisfy people who quite possibly don't care about what you do with your life? Stop wasting time impressing others, keeping up with the Jones', or comparing yourself to others. It is not worth it, and all your effort will not pay off.

10. **You have dreams but don't think you are worthy of them.**

    a. You may feel shame or guilt about taking a risk and it not working out. The possibility is always there that it may not work out, but so is the possibility that it will. Flip the narrative and ask yourself if you would be proud of yourself for guaranteeing that it doesn't work out.

b. Low self-esteem is the main culprit here. The only remedy to this is to dive deep with the help of a professional, whether a well-trained expert coach or therapist, if necessary, to explore the patterns and causes and then develop solutions to strengthen your self-esteem. Here again, your desire to change must be greater than your desire to stay the same.

"We may encounter many defeats, but we must not be defeated."- Maya Angelou

The upside to failure: Whoa, what? How could there possibly be an upside to failure?

"Success is a lousy teacher. It seduces smart people into thinking they can't lose." – Bill Gates

Failure is never about smarts. Smart people fail all the time. Failure is a part of life and should not be feared. Even for the most talented of us, there's no question that we'll fail. It's a matter of when and how we respond. Here are a small sampling of firmly held beliefs by smart leaders that proved wrong and a few well-known products born out of failures.

- "I think there is a world market for maybe five computers" – Thomas Watson, Chairman, IBM 1943 (they failed to see the market shifting and the beginning trend toward miniaturization.)
- "This telephone has too many shortcomings to be seriously considered as a means of communication. The device is inherently of no value to us." – Western Union internal memo, 1876 (they stayed behind and never caught up with communication competitors.)
- "There is no reason why anyone would want a computer in their home." – Ken Olsen, Founder, Digital Equipment Corp. (DEC) 1977 (completely ignored and missed the PC market.)
- Viagra was a failed cardiovascular therapeutic that had an interesting side effect.
- The Post-It Note from 3M was a failed adhesive.
- Bubble wrap was invented as a 3D wallpaper but never took off.
- The mouthwash Listerine was initially intended as a surgical antiseptic.
- The Pacemaker was an accidental invention initially created to record the sound of the human heart.

Failures are not what defines you,
but not ever trying does.

Failure is never permanent except in the wide world of sports, but don't forget that the next season provides another opportunity for a comeback. John C. Maxwell promotes the concept of "Fail early, fail often, but always fail forward." A concept popularized in startups and venture capital communities.

Experiencing failure stings, and the more the ego is involved, the more painful the sting. Yet, it is infinitely better than living with the regret of not having tried. In fact, not taking chances or smart risks is among the top ten regrets that people cite on their deathbeds. "I wish I would've done this, or tried this, or not held myself back from...."

This reminds me of the story by Les Brown, Emmy Award-Winning motivational speaker, who makes this point perfectly:

> "Imagine a world where if you are laying on your death bed, the ghosts of every idea, every dream you had, the abilities, the talent given to you by life and that you, for whatever reason, never acted on those ideas, you never pursued that dream, you never used those talents, you never used your voice, never wrote that book. And there they are, standing around your bed looking at you with large angry eyes saying, 'We came to you, and only you could've given us life. And now, we must die with you forever."

Trust me, the sting of failure disappears much quicker than the years of regret you endure because your brain and soul will not let you forget. Succumbing to the fear of failing at something is useless when you could instead be applauding yourself for having the courage to try because this is where you feel the aliveness in your soul.

The only failure you should fear is NOT knowing yourself.

The mindset that kills the seed of confidence – Earlier, I touched on our tendency to do anything to avoid being wrong. But what if we're wrong about that? "Wrongologist" Kathryn Schulz makes a compelling case for not just admitting but embracing our fallibility.[50] Assumptions occur when others have the same generally shared information and still think differently. Here are a few that should be avoided:

- The notion that getting something wrong means there is something wrong with you.
- Expectations, given and perceived. Example: trusting too much in feelings of your version of righteousness as being on the correct side of anything This could become a dangerous premise, leaving no room for other perspectives.
- We stop entertaining the possibility that we could be wrong. That's when we make costly mistakes because we didn't do the work of developing systems thinking.

---

50 https://www.ted.com/talks/kathryn_schulz_on_being_wrong

Another mindset that can kill the seed of confidence is when we fall into a **comfort trap** where we're stuck, refusing or avoiding challenging ourselves. We are most comfortable with that which is familiar to us. This is because we grew up learning that the unfamiliar was not to be trusted. Parents typically teach kids not to talk to strangers. To not try anything that could harm them. To not be different and instead fit in. These are all well-intentioned lessons that shape a person's foundation. The familiarity of that mindset becomes safe. It becomes comfortable. So why would anyone want to disrupt such pleasant comfort?

Build resilience by challenging your internal status quo.

If you refuse to lose, you haven't failed.

I offer these ideas and concepts throughout this book because they are grounded on first challenging your internal status quo.

If you believe that it is better to go with 'the devil you know', then you are in the comfort trap. Ask yourself, what is the 'reward' you are getting by staying in that comfort? Is it possibly just confirming your identity as someone who doesn't deserve the possibility of success by taking a chance? Is this comfort an excuse to avoid experiencing a future fear of failing? Is it fueling another insecurity so much that you'd rather pretend you don't want a better life?

If you believe you first need confidence before you take a chance on something, know that confidence is not something you just wish for, or even use willpower to make it appear. It takes effort, courage, time, and practice—lots of it. Therefore, confidence is a by-product of continually trying new things and marveling at your improvement. You are never an imposter if you are learning.

Start taking note of any of these counterproductive behaviors and stop them in their tracks. Ask yourself, are you:

- Avoiding your emotions?
- Harshly judging your thoughts?
- Rehashing the past?
- Fearfully anticipating the future?
- Acting impulsively?

Trying to ignore your thoughts and feelings does not help. Instead, accept them and view them with curiosity. What can you learn from them? Then think about what you truly care about in life. I often use this quote with my clients who struggle with confidence and fear of failure.

"While one person hesitates because they feel inferior; the other is busy making mistakes and becoming superior." – Henry C Link, Psychologist

It helps to accept that you cannot fabricate or will confidence. And you can never achieve confidence by simply thinking about it. You must take action. The more action and the more failings, the more your mind expands to incorporate these lessons into the next move. By not committing yourself to reframing failure and the fear that holds you back, you miss out on that opportunity by not acting.

Building confidence requires you to be brutally honest with yourself. This does not mean you should beat yourself up whenever you mess up. It means being watchful for the counterproductive behaviors I mentioned above. Ensure you are not setting little traps for yourself that sabotage your chances of achieving what you want. Perhaps it is best to prioritize getting help to break those unconscious self-sabotage habits if those behaviors show up.

We should also not discount that, many times, success is often just a matter of luck, and all you can do is increase your odds or probability of succeeding. Of course, the operative phrase is 'increasing your odds'- there are always things you can do to impact the results. Remember, *"Chance favors the prepared mind."* - Louis Pasteur.

Food for the soul relating to failure

There is a lot we can learn from ancient philosophers, and while I continue to seek ways to integrate the teachings of Socrates (know thyself), I also find the wisdom of the

Stoics like Marcus Aurelius and others to be a source of grounding and centering. They inspire me and are woven into my personal and business values that guide everything that I do

Contrary to my usual patterns and preferences, I attended a lecture from Dr. Srikumar Rao, known for his TED Talk on happiness and the course he developed at Columbia University. The course was so powerful that it was said that Rao's students came out as warriors of their own lives. Now, there's an attention grabber.

The syllabus outright states: "I expect that this course will profoundly change your life. If it does not, then we have both failed."

In his story, he says, *"My program changes lives because the ideas and concepts I propagate were taken from great masters who completely understood the human predicament and came up with solutions to the dilemmas we face. They have been tested over millennia, and they absolutely work."*

"When I run after what I think I want, my days are a furnace of stress and anxiety; if I sit in my own place of patience, what I need flows to me, and without pain. From this, I understand that what I want also wants me, is looking for me and attracting me. There is a great secret here for anyone who can grasp it." Rumi – a great 13th-century Sufi philosopher and poet.

Interestingly, Rao's teachings correlate with false and dysfunctional mindsets I've witnessed where people mistakenly believe that success gives you happiness, and if they fail, there is something wrong with them. This thinking only reveals their rigid expectations of how things should be or work, but the real world does not agree.

"You don't have control, you never had control, you will never have control." - Srikuma Rao

Hearing this made me think, wait a minute, I have always been a control freak, so where does that leave me!? The fact is that the only things I had control over were my actions and decisions.

Rao continues, "When you consciously give up control, you actually achieve more control."

Whoa, say what? Are you feeling like a bomb just exploded in your brain? I sure did when I first heard it. It challenged many of my beliefs, and I had to unpack this carefully. This point made me even more curious.

I thought about it this way: collision of innovation – like a rubric cause-and-effect model. It also reminded me of the first programming language I learned – Basic – which applied the if-then-else logic. This early programming logic gave me scenario-planning skills and testing hypotheses in everything I did and observed. It gave me the advantage of navigating my career trajectories and being more prepared and less taken by surprise. Unsurprisingly, analyzing behavioral patterns also applies a similar logic, the law of consequence.

Yet, when it comes to drawing conclusions or forming theories from my research, what intrigued me most about researching technology trends and behaviors was the elusive problem of the chicken and the egg – which came first?

I've spent decades researching and observing technology adoption cycles, behaviors, and generational trends, and, with fascination, trying to solve for them as if they were an equation. Maybe I was motivated to find other ways to have more control over my life, future, and my family's well-being. This mindset was deeply ingrained in my upbringing because I knew I could not count on my mom or siblings to support my dreams, so I only had myself to depend on if I was going to break the chains of poverty.

By attending this session with Dr. Rao, I intentionally invited the possibility of being wrong and expanding my perspective. I learned that what I called control was really all actions I could take to increase my odds of achieving my goals, but not control of the outcomes. It further confirmed the traps we often fall into because of semantics and the definitions or judgments about what occurs as we live our lives. But that is the purpose of our brain, to make sense of the world and do predictive body budgeting.

When I was done, I felt grateful for these valuable insights because just allowing them into my brain and heart seemed to take a weight off my back. And boy, I felt energized. My clients tell me they get this feeling when I help them learn to let go of unwarranted fears that have shackled them for years. This is why I love what I do.

If you found some nuggets of wisdom that have inspired you to open your mind to learning and exploring it, then this book is a success. It would have been a guaranteed failure had I not published it at all.

I'll leave you to ponder on this. How will you serve the world? What does the world need that your talent can provide? When you figure it out, you will have succeeded.

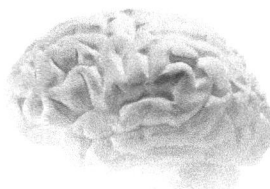

CHAPTER 8

SELF-MASTERY TO SUCCESS

Let's address the elephant in the room: *What if I don't want to improve myself?*

If you are reading this book and have asked yourself that question, the next best question is, *"Where is this coming from?"* If we were working together, I'd ask you why this thought came up for you. Are you experiencing days when your motivation feels nonexistent? Envisioning having to do a bunch of heavy lifting in prescriptive practices or digging deep to understand how your brain is or is not working for you might seem daunting. The idea of facing deep-seated fears or buried ghosts you don't want to meet is enough to say, *Thank you, but no thank you.*

I know exactly how that feels. I've been there many times, and I know it will happen again because I am human. Setting high expectations for myself and achieving success does not mean I don't have moments like these. I used to power through it, using every ounce of pure willpower I had. From this, I either got a payout or a case of burnout. A payout was when I gained something from that heroic effort. It felt good, and I felt validated in my strategy and sacrifice. The burnout was when I got nothing, nada, zero, out of it. I had wasted time and energy running on fumes, only to realize I had gone in the wrong direction. Ouch. It was a bitter pill to swallow, knowing I was running on empty until the next time I could find the time to recharge my batteries, but only ever enough to continue.

For many years I was a self-improvement junkie. I used self-improvement as a way to deal with my insecurities. Don't get me wrong, many benefits are gained, but when insecurities are the fuel that drives your motivation, you will find yourself in an exhausting vicious cycle because your insecurities will still be there, even if you succeed.

If you relate or it sounds familiar because you or someone you know suffers because of it, the first thing I'll tell you is that it is not your fault. It was never your fault, and it will never be your fault. It is your untrained brain working against you. I knew I had to find a better way to improve my odds for a good payout and avoid burnout. Throughout this book, I've included valuable insights and tips, but here, you'll find things you can do right away, others I recommend pursuing, and mistakes to avoid in your journey. You'll also find more stories with significant human impact.

Self-improvement mistakes to avoid

Focusing on technology and behavioral trends, I always looked at innovation-driven tools and techniques to improve my performance and be more precise on what was vital for managing the ever-growing challenges the future held for me. Decades of being on this journey taught me that I would've been much better off if I had first invested in learning how to throttle myself more intelligently and strategically. Even worse, the 'payouts' I got were sometimes not as good as I had expected and, metaphorically, not tax-free. I paid a heavy tax on the impact on loved ones, colleagues, and anyone else in my path. False truths abound. There is also no such thing as quick success, overnight enlightenment, or instant motivation. The same thing goes for the numerous personality tests that claim to tell you who you are. I tried many of them and researched the rest.

According to Dr. Lisa Feldman Barrett, personality assessments have no more scientific validity than horoscopes. Years of evidence show that the popular Myers-Briggs Type Indicator (MBTI) does not live up to its claims and does not consistently predict job performance. Yet, otherwise capable managers get lured into making decisions that benefit neither their team nor their company.

She posits that the results seem real because the questions ask you about your beliefs about yourself. The bottom line is that you can't measure behavior by asking people their opinions about their behavior. Furthermore, that behavior could be different in multiple contexts. A person could be introverted in one context but extroverted in others. Not all assessments are created equal!

With myriad assessment tool providers, it can be daunting to choose the best solution. Some assessment providers stand on the laurels of research done 20 or 30 years ago, while others constantly evaluate nuances and stay on the cutting edge. When considering an assessment provider, always ask for research findings and published papers, preferably peer-reviewed reports. Assessment companies that use science-based assessments engender more confidence than those that create and distribute them based on hunches or receive some marketing buzz. Ask if they have a validation study associated with their instrument. It's best if conducted by independent statisticians for objective purposes, from data norming to data analysis to structured equation sampling.

The good news is that there is a better way to deal with insecurities and other obstacles that get in the way of achieving your goals. I've had great success with my clients who implement my methods and techniques aside what it has done for me. My life has never been better, happier, and more fulfilled than it is now. This is why I chose to make this the best gift I can give the world.

If you do nothing else, take these interim reboot steps:

Honor yourself: This means being honest and authentic to yourself. Take the time you need to reflect, but in a relaxed way, not as a task to be done. It makes a difference. What kind of life do you want for yourself and your loved ones?

Watch your cognitive capacity: Our brains, like our bodies, need to replenish when overworked. Without it, cognitive functioning will decline or shut down.

Forgive yourself: If you lean towards obsessively looping over thoughts that sound like, "I must, but I can't," you will place yourself in high cognitive dissonance. Don't beat yourself up through mental self-flagellation because that's like adding fuel to the fire.

Gift yourself a different perspective:

o   Self-improvement is not something you *have* to do if you don't want to. It should be something you *get* to do. If you are happy with every aspect of your life (and you are not in denial or settling), don't force yourself.

o   *"If you get tired, learn to rest, not to quit."* -Banksy

o   Instead of saying, "One day I'll be good enough," say, "I'm good enough, but I want to be better."

o   *"Beware of false knowledge; it is more dangerous than ignorance."* – George Bernard Shaw.

o   Spend less time in your head and more time interacting. This is something I worked hard to cultivate in myself. You see, I was all in when I was playing, having a blast. I was also all in when I was working, which meant intense concentration on problem-solving activities, but I left little room for quality relationships.

On the other hand, if you decided to skip all the previous chapters because you are looking for a 'quick fix,' you are either unaware of your blind spots or actively self-sabotaging. In Chapter 5 I explained how this behavior impacts you and those around you. Please know this is not a judgment. I've mastered the art of being non-judgmental. My profession also demands this of me. If you were my client, I'd ask you to consider whether this is the best thing you can do for yourself or whether you may be doing yourself a disservice.

This chapter is for those serious about getting in the driver's seat toward success and learning to survive and thrive in a VUCA world. Doing so is no longer a luxury but a necessity because VUCA will continue to increase the number and magnitude of human challenges. It is for people who want a better, more fulfilled life for themselves, their loved ones, their business, profession, or community, and those who wish to positively impact and leave a legacy for future generations.

It takes motivation

"People often say that motivation doesn't last. Well, neither does bathing—that's why we recommend it daily."—Zig Ziglar

Embarking on a journey to becoming a better leader in business and life, a person you'd admire, requires time, energy, and patience. Changing thought patterns seems challenging, but it is more possible than you think. To be clear, this is not a solo sport. If your leadership career or personal life is not going how you want, you need objective, trusted guidance and the best tools available to create clarity and align your values and purpose. Your desire to change for the better must be stronger than your desire to stay the same. If it isn't, you signal that you've become comfortably numb to your status quo and have possibly given up on yourself. That would be tragic, but it does not have to be that way.

I spent my whole life waging war against the status quo. Had I not, I would've remained in poverty, not have the loving, supportive family I have, and would still be blaming others for how my life turned out. The things around you won't change unless you change the things around you. Stephen R. Covey may have said it best when he stated, *"I am not a product of my circumstances. I am a product of my decisions."*

Before COVID-19, this quote conveyed accountability, ownership, and no excuses. Living by this made me feel both liberated and powerful. I invested in training on the Stephen Covey methods and mindsets even though I had already adopted many of them from the school of hard knocks called life. I did this because I knew I could learn much more from different perspectives. I was right. We all felt the impact of the pandemic, and it's not our doing. In preparation for a speaking engagement during COVID-19, I analyzed this quote to test whether it still applied in that context. The answer is yes! Despite the pandemic, circumstances still don't make us who we are; every decision we make still does. It is more about how we show up and what we do with the information we have. For example, are you using systems thinking to understand the interaction between the components that comprise the entirety of a designed system and not just the sum of the components? How do you currently respond during a crisis? Is your self-perception aligned with others' perception of you during challenging times?

The great news is that we can do better for ourselves – it's called neuroplasticity.

The medical definition of neuroplasticity is the brain's ability to reorganize itself by forming new neural connections throughout life.[51]

---

51   https://www.medicinenet.com/neuroplasticity/definition.htm

According to the <u>National Library of Medicine</u>, the first mention of the term plasticity regarding the nervous system was by William James in 1890.[52] However, the term neural plasticity is credited to Jerzy Konorski in 1948,[53] and popularized by Donald Hebb in 1949.[54]

Neuroplasticity, or brain plasticity, is a response to experiences from which neural connections form and ultimately build patterns as the brain makes sense of the outside world. This activity only stops the moment you die. From the time you are born, your brain develops neural connections that, with practice, shape who you become. As a newborn, you discover the world visually, but all you have is a lantern by which to see. As you grow, more and more of the world comes into focus as the lantern becomes a flashlight. These are neurons firing together to give meaning to everything around you through all your organ sensors that encompass all your thoughts, experiences, feelings, and actions and have the potential to sculpt the neurocircuits they travel through. We're training our brains from birth. Neuroplasticity occurs quickly in young brains because the neurons in the cerebral cortex go from 2,500 neurons at birth to 15,000 by age three. Everything about the world experienced during these first three years is new to the various senses, whether it is sounds you

52   Berlucchi G, Buchtel HA. Neuronal plasticity: historical roots and evolution of meaning. Exp Brain Res. 2009 Jan;192(3):307-19.

53   Mateos-Aparicio P, Rodríguez-Moreno A. The Impact of Studying Brain Plasticity. Front Cell Neurosci. 2019;13:66

54   Josselyn SA, Köhler S, Frankland PW. Heroes of the Engram. J Neurosci. 2017 May 03;37(18):4647-4657.

hear (auditory), what you taste (gustatory), what you see (visual), what you touch (kinesthetic), and what you smell (olfactory).

The brain takes in every experience indiscriminately. As you grow into adulthood, the number of neuronal synapses decreases because of synaptic pruning. Synaptic pruning occurs as you develop and strengthen some connections and prune weaker ones that are not used often. However, the experience element beyond the sensors more profoundly shapes the structure and function of the brain as brain development is activity-dependent to establish pathways for different hierarchies of brain function. It means every electrical activity in every circuit – sensory, motor, emotional, cognitive – shapes the way circuits get together. Changes and learning become a passive and natural process for the brain.

Older brains are also plastic, but changes and learning tend to become more challenging when the learning muscles have not been exercised enough – similar to the muscles in your body. Use them or lose them. The good news is that this is reversible under the right conditions and motivations. The willingness to practice adaptability first is crucial in accelerating progress in all other areas of learning to stimulate new neural connections for mindset and paradigm shifts. In the airport analogy, it is like creating new flight routes to get the passengers to their destination when the original route is no longer available.

Exercising your brain for adaptability is like becoming a good swimmer. The better you get, the more water you can explore without being limited to the shallow end of a pool. You can swim in the ocean and lakes and feel confident trying water sports like waterskiing, windsurfing, and more. It gives you leverage and opportunity that you would otherwise not have if you weren't willing to be adaptable.

My daughter, Nikita, had no trouble adapting to a new environment in a large university because she had already experienced several corporate relocations and schools in earlier years. She learned to see it as an opportunity to make new friends and explore new campuses and that our family was the constant support system. When we moved from the Bay Area in California to San Diego, a 4th-grade teacher remarked how impressed she was with Nikita because *"she was so comfortable in her own skin."* A true sign of adaptability and good self-esteem. Nikita would build upon her experience and develop patterns of thinking that wherever she went, it was only a matter of figuring out how things worked in that environment, who's who, making new friends, and doing her best. The move to Washington state was just as smooth, so by the time she went away to a major university, she was strategically minded because she had been training her brain to work for her and not against her. My perspective growing up was entirely different as I didn't have the same support system we gave Nikita.

I had to become self-reliant and adopt the core perseverance attitude often reflected in the military mantra 'Improvise, Adapt, Overcome.' Improvise with what you have at hand, adapt to new and unexpected changes, and overcome obstacles in all situations: same outcome, different approaches to train for adaptability. Nikita's was fostered via externally driven experiences but with support. Mine was internally driven experiences developed for survival because of the lack of support. The point is that regardless of your experience, you can improve your adaptability primarily by actively practicing putting yourself in different situations, picking up new skills, or setting new routines. Building your adaptability muscle enhances your ability to develop the right combination of insight and foresight. It starts with understanding how your brain works. You can improve your ability to improvise when you become armed with the right skills and tools, vastly improving your odds of overcoming anything life throws at you.

The danger of inaction

The brain is astonishing and always figuring out ways to maintain the body's functional and cognitive resources. If you don't adequately exercise your brain, old patterns become cemented and not refreshed as the world changes. This means that old patterns and biases take a dominant position by sinking into the unconscious, making them even harder to detect and contributing to more and more blind spots. The brain is exceptional at constantly tuning and pruning its complex neurocircuitry as I described earlier. Neurons that no longer fire together are removed in the same way that dead branches are pruned from a tree. Neuroscientists call this brain activity tuning and pruning, supporting findings that our brain continues to be shaped and reshaped in adulthood. In practical terms, neurocircuits for attributes like curiosity, a sense of adventure, and mental agility are ultimately pruned.

"We don't stop playing because we grow old. We grow old because we stop playing." – George Bernard Shaw

Too many people live with fear and make fear-based decisions. This is one of the biggest mistakes leaders make, and they make it without even realizing it. Why is this? Because they either don't have experience or were never trained to lead during a crisis. Don't get me wrong, not all fear is bad, as I unpacked fear in Chapter 2. The point is to have a healthy relationship with fear and other emotions that often get in the way of our own success.

Here's how I help

There is so much suffering in the world, and it is expressed in a million different ways because we are all unique. Having faced and conquered many adversities, I understand the pain others are going through and can identify the areas that need to heal and those that need to be fortified. I'm grateful to have amassed a multidisciplinary, multifunctional, and multi-industry background that has kept me at the forefront of innovation. My services and programs employ a strategic combination of brain science, skills development, and art. Yes, I said art. It is not a one-size-fits-all solution because people are not clones (at least not in the flesh yet that I know of!)

With all the disruptions I discussed in Chapter 4 accumulating and aggregating, we are left with a growing set of mental health challenges. What makes this situation worse is the stigma associated with mental health issues, which keeps so many people from seeking help. It is critical to know that mental illnesses such as depression are *not* a personal failure. I'll say it again, it is not your fault. The only failure is how society has responded to people afflicted with mental health disorders. Without the proper systems, tools, and guidance, people get into a state of Disruption Fatigue (DF). What is DF? Disruption Fatigue is the culmination of living in a VUCA world which often leads to mental health issues such as depression, anxiety, trauma, and stressor-related health issues. I listed examples of disruptions in business and in life and noted that the pandemic impacted both the professional and personal areas of our lives. Its impact presents similar to PTSD, post-traumatic stress disorder and its symptoms in that it is event-driven and prolonged stress-induced. I also emphasized that as sure as death and taxes, disruptions will occur.

By now you're likely thinking that this disruption thing is a bad thing but that is not the case. When you are innovating and growing (yourself or your business), disruption feels good because you are adding to or improving something by replacing the old with the new. It feels good when it is self-directed and leads to improved outcomes and goals achieved. The flipside is when you are the one being disrupted and it does not serve you, it feels bad, making way for the belief that someone or something else is to blame. This is zero-sum thinking that leads to misery and prolonged pain.

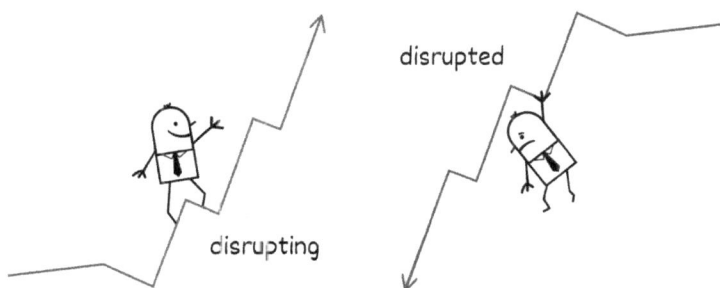

If people spent more time disrupting themselves in the right way, they would spend less time being disrupted. So, why don't they? Most people subconsciously avoid being their own disruptor because change can be uncomfortable, and people avoid discomfort even to their own detriment. This is an example of your brain working against you. Disrupting yourself takes effort and energy, and the last thing you want is more work and effort when all you want to do is relax, check social media, watch your favorite television programs, shop for things you don't really need, and hang out with friends.

My 3-Step Brain Empowerment Blueprint

The brain is the architect of your experience. This is why I directed my research to cognitive functioning or brain science. How our brains develop is perfectly explained in a two-minute video created by the National Scientific Council on the Developing Child at Harvard University.[55] Brains reply on the patterns they have built from our experiences, so when there are none and uncertainty is the only certainty, it's very stressful for us. So, it is no wonder we, meaning our brains, suffer so much. As adults, we face many life and professional disruptions, such as the ones I discussed in Chapter 4. As they accumulate over time or aggregate over a short time, they cause wear and tear damage to your brain, affecting your performance. Similar to your car – its brakes, tires, fluids, and systems affect its performance, making it more challenging to arrive at your destination if they are not well maintained.

My greatest joy is to guide and assist knowledge professionals and leaders in becoming the people they most admire and would want to be; to master every aspect of themselves in a way that they are adaptable, mentally dexterous, emotionally intelligent, VUCA-resilient, and

---

55 https://developingchild.harvard.edu/resources/project-for-ba-bies/

wiser decision-makers. I help them become people who can detect, synthesize, and be strategic when faced with the rapid pace of unforeseen disruptive changes that come with the VUCA world. These are the things that block their success. With a specialty in brain science, I empower clients with proprietary systems and tools to help them regain their competitive advantage. I've synthesized my life's work into a 3-Step Brain Empowerment Blueprint where my clients learn to **Discover, Decode, and Design** guided success strategies tailored to their primary goals. This proven methodology is part of the Human-First Performance Systems™ (HFPS) I developed to help current and future leaders thrive in a VUCA world. My HFPS system will help you to:

1. Discover your powers and new ways to get ahead of shifting trends and anticipate disruptions by learning systems-thinking techniques.

2. Design evergreen plans and practices to engage and lead yourself and your teams more effectively, even during challenging times, giving you a continued return on investment (ROI).

3. Deploy strategies to increase your mental resiliency, adaptability, and agility by applying systems-thinking approaches for wiser decision-making, delivering a roadmap to building new patterns for success.

The results are real, impactful, and powerful because the system makes you more responsive, less reactive, and more future-ready. For example:

-   Leaders benefit from resiliency, adaptability, EQ, and strategic thinking, measuring up to 80% increased confidence, average productivity increase by 38%, increased efficiency, improved business management by 61%, and greater employee productivity by 37%.

-   Teams benefit from improved productivity and reduced stress, measuring up to 51% improved team effectiveness, improved interpersonal relationships by 73%, better outcomes – higher quality by 26%, and improved productivity by 37%.

-   Companies benefit from becoming a leading, sought-after company for top talent when applied company-wide. They will see improved customer loyalty by up to 50%, increased motivation to be 1st to market by 46%, higher sales by up to 50%, increased agility to meet future demands, and higher profits by up to 27%.

How it works:

Discover

Discovering who you are on a deeper level is the most important gift you can give yourself. It leads to releasing trapped emotions that you may have been holding onto for decades and freeing yourself of the baggage you have been carrying. Consider it an investment in yourself, the safest investment you can make because you will not only see and feel rapid results, but the benefits of investing in yourself will continue to pay dividends for the rest of your life. **Why do I say that? Because you take yourself wherever you go.**

Humans have the most complex and integrative brains of all living things. The three-pound organ is the seat of intelligence, interpreter of the senses, initiator of body movement, and controller of behavior. So much happens that we are not consciously aware of. The Discover step of my Brain Empowerment Blueprint uncovers crucial elements of your patterns, self-perception, goals, problem-solving habits, and more. Guided sessions and neuroscience-backed tools bring hidden talents into focus and put them to work for you. You learn how you do what you do and why you do what you do. Once you achieve clarity of self, you immediately feel more empowered. Imagine trying to read a map through a cloudy window. It is difficult to see where exactly you are at any time. You can't see the area's details to determine the best path to your desired destination. Essentially you are moving through the world blindfolded. Scary.

Here's an example of critical questions you'll be able to answer for yourself with confidence like never before.

#1 How do you show up during a crisis?

That fact is that most people haven't trained their brains to be responsive instead of reactive. Therefore, people tend to have an ideal vision of what they do or would do. The reality is that they have no idea if they have not experienced a crisis before. Running out of your favorite espresso in the morning does not constitute a crisis. When stressed or overwhelmed, we are in the perfect state to make bad decisions. During a crisis, you may experience a rush of adrenaline, reacting in a state of fright, flight, or fight. Unmanaged fear emotions can lead you astray and cause negative behaviors such as abandoning the team, freezing and being unable to communicate, blaming others, and forgetting procedures or processes in a state of panic.

#2 How adaptable are you?

In our increasingly disruptive world, *"It is not the strongest of the species that survives, nor the most intelligent, but the one most responsive to change."* – Charles Darwin. Many factors stand in the way of becoming more adaptable. These factors can range from the hierarchy in your organization, fear, decision bias, entrenched habits, a skills defic t, short-term thinking, rigid practices and structures, lack of diversity, and lack of clarity and purpose. Being adaptable is not something you can just turn on or off at will. It requires building new habits, not chasing immediate results. On average, forming a new habit can take around two to three months, but it can vary widely depending on the behavior you are trying to change, the individual, and the circumstances.

Sustaining the habit is yet another challenge. If you want to change your life forever, you'll benefit from learning how to learn and also learning how you learn. Understand which mental models you use, and which ones you should adopt. This ability alone will increase your motivation, make you more adaptable, relatable, and exciting, and help you get better jobs and earn more money. An important factor to remember is that during challenging times that heighten or prolong stress, the brain defaults to previous bad habits, just like weeds can come back and grow when you don't tend to your garden on a regular basis.

#3 Do you know your confidence and skill gap scores?

Gaps in confidence are often rooted in fear, as discussed in Chapters 2 and 7. Identifying them is a critical step in designing the plans to close the gaps. It has nothing to do with intellect or capacity. It is crucial to avoid the 'false confidence' trap you keep yourself in to keep from looking weak to others or facing your fears. This also comes in to play with the belief that you must 'fake it 'til you make it.' This can work as a mantra to summon the courage to try something new that is outside your comfort zone, such as public speaking, but not as a way to navigate through life. When you avoid doing discovery work, you do yourself and those around you more harm than good. Deluding yourself only sets you up for painful emotions when tested. Think of confidence as a balloon that bursts at the slightest pinprick. Brene Brown says perfectionism is *"...the belief that if we live perfectly, look perfectly, and act perfectly, we can avoid the pain of blame, judgment, and shame."*

#4 Have you examined your knowing/doing gap?

Highly intelligent people often have the most significant knowing/doing gaps. In practice, this is when you know what you should do and how but don't, or what you shouldn't do but do anyway. They misguidedly fail to understand that: Knowing what's right doesn't mean much unless you do what's right. This is not to be seen as accountability shaming but rather a self-sabotage pattern. It is critical to analyze this because the seed of building true confidence is in the act of doing. When I work with clients, once the gaps are discovered, we work on addressing the underlying patterns responsible for the gaps.

In Chapter 4, I shared my car accident story, which resulted in my bout with depression. I took hard lessons from the incident that fall into this knowing/doing gap.

1. Don't do the right things for (what you *believe* is) the right reason (i.e. the show must go on). I knew this, but I was in denial and misguided.

2. Trying to tough it out for too long do you no favors. Don't take yourself for granted. I knew this, but I allowed myself to develop hypertension from prolonged high stress, and I was a heart attack waiting to happen. I was biased by thinking I was tougher than I was.

3. You won't go wrong investing in yourself, especially to reclaim your **better self**. I could've saved myself almost a year of suffering if only I sought help sooner. What if I had that heart attack and left my kids motherless and my husband a widower because my blind spots kept me from making smart decisions? Once I sought help, I learned about avoidance coping and how that is a form of self-sabotage.

4. For patience's sake, close the knowing/doing gap. Knowing and doing are *not* the same. I knew this intellectually and previously looked down on people who would 'talk the talk' but not 'walk the walk.' Then I found myself in that trap without being aware of it and only later realized how that happened.

Whether I'm presenting on stages or working with private clients, my primary focus is to reduce the pain and suffering they experience and guide them towards closing their knowing/doing gaps and preventing self-sabotage.

#5 Do you trust your team, and do they trust you?

This one is extremely difficult because trust is difficult to analyze. When we assume that trust is dependent entirely on the behavior of others, we fall short as leaders. Extensive surveys from employees and managers show a significant spread between the perception of trust and what defines it as it relates to almost every question asked ranging from understanding the vision of the company to meeting the needs of employees to the readiness of their talent, the effectiveness of communication, and more. Trust is critical for organizational health and need not be elusive. My *Team Effectiveness* program helps teams and leaders achieve trust and regain harmony and productivity.

Other sample discovery topics that are foundational and critical success factors where I provide guidance include:

Are you practicing avoidance coping over previous traumas or during a conflict?

Avoidance coping is a maladaptive form of coping, forcing behaviors that stop you from thinking about or facing feelings or memories that make you uncomfortable. This is also a form of self-sabotage.

Whether you realize it or not, your relationships are negatively impacted. Because it is a stressor, your health is affected, weakening your immune system, exacerbating skin conditions, or messing with your hormones. It can also lead to neck and back problems. You also reinforce unproductive and self-sabotaging habits and emotions like fear, relying on hope when hope is not a strategy, determining the future based on past experiences, and, most importantly, undermining happiness. My *Self-Leadership* program empowers you to detect and prevent this behavior and to instead respond more effectively and confidently in any situation.

How much are you relying on gut feelings and instincts? When are you most aware of them?

As a business leader, I often used my gut feelings as part of my decision-making process. Every leader that I speak with proudly says they follow their gut feelings. Gut feelings or intuition are overrated because they are too often tainted with psychological and cognitive biases, blind spots, limiting beliefs, fears, or other emotions that hold you back or lead you astray. Neuroscientists recognize that most people's intuition and gut feelings are emotionally driven and discourage us from simply dismissing them. Therefore, in every state, it is wise to consider whether your intuition has correctly assessed the situation. Part of my discovery approach calls for exploring and leveraging the driving forces because they are appraisals of what you have experienced, making them a rich system for information processing. So, it is not about eliminating emotions from the decision-making process; it's about taming and directing them by first assessing and recognizing those emotions or over-rationalized thoughts that may be faulty. I've learned over the decades that there is not just one master (no one ring that rules them all!) in decision-making. You need to be kind to yourself and understand that your heart wants to lead you to happiness but won't if it is misguided.

The brain, however, can also be misguided if it ignores or overrides the heart altogether. So, when making decisions, whether you are more brain-driven or heart-driven, make sure to bring them both into play. Your odds of success significantly increase when they are both in the best shape they can be. **The exception** regarding gut feelings and intuition is that **only the purest intuitions are always right**. This is the driving force behind guiding leaders toward uncovering them first and then creating strategies to remove the enemies of big goals.

An example of pure intuition is in Chapter 7 where I talk about the power behind my burning desire to escape poverty expressed in actions I took which I playfully described as 'what-was-I-thinking moments.' With the proper neuroscience-validated tools, I help clients learn to recognize when their brain is in overdrive or ruminating mode and how to overcome it. This occurs when worry and any of its derivatives are uncovered.

Decode

Everything around us is changing. Therefore, you can either adapt and become future-proof or stay where you are and become obsolete. The most successful companies, organizations, and teams are the ones that have a strong learning culture. Strong learning cultures outperform the competition. With my Human-first Performance Systems (HPS), you and your teams can become up to:

- 46% more innovative
- 37% more efficient
- 58% more agile
- 26% improved quality

Designing a strong learning culture for your organization, team, and individuals is the key to elevating and achieving this performance. The first step is to develop the vision and then the roadmap to get there, which is co-created and guided every step of the way. Developing a vision is not recommended as a solo sport. Doing it yourself will only lead to wasted time and resources, or finding yourself enthusiastically running in the wrong direction. This is because it is one of the hardest things to articulate, especially because it requires digging deep for that vision; otherwise, it will fail and create cognitive dissonance. Cognitive dissonance is the mental conflict that occurs when a person's behaviors, beliefs, or values do not align. It may also happen when a person holds two beliefs that contradict one another.

> *"If you are not progressing, you*
> *are regressing." – Elon Musk.*

Next is to use the information gathered, assessed, and integrated with the desired vision or goals and create the details to fill in the roadmap and co-create the action plan. What skills and habits need to be forged or fortified? Keep in mind that habits, like Rome, are not built in a day, and the only way to make them sustainable is to focus on what you can do daily. I always recommend starting with a couple of needle movers. Typically, these are critical paths to achieving other gains faster, so they must be carefully modeled and digestible for you and directed through daily practices. Success depends on building a habit that will ignite and maintain your motivation. It does not happen by itself. You need to cultivate it.

Design

Execution is everything. All the best prep in the world will not yield the results you want if you are not taking action. Imagine adapting, improvising, and overcoming disruptive challenges like a well-trained Navy Seal that stays calm during the most dangerous and challenging missions where a mistake can cost them and others their lives. Imagine being more responsive and less reactive. Imagine being in the driver's seat of your life, career, or business instead of the back seat, letting the enemies of your goals take the driver's seat. Whatever the challenge, my systems, programs, and training empower you to get firmly in the driver's seat and let your self-defeating emotions and negative self-talk take the passenger seat. They are no longer in charge. This means you are aware of them, acknowledge them, and make a well-informed decision on the best action to take for yourself. For example, when it comes to managing VUCA, I teach you how to take the bull by the horns. The skills and techniques you learn will turn:

Volatility into Vision, **U**ncertainty into Understanding, **C**omplexity into Clarity, **A**mbiguity into Agility.

In my programs, this is what I mean when I talk about the ability to strategically design solutions that combine the gold standard in coaching modalities with advanced skills training to turn threats into opportunities. The ROI can be in the ten-fold range when you consider that you can apply my systems to all areas of your business and personal life, whether challenges arise tomorrow, next year, or in the future. Even better, this is where you begin closing your Knowing/Doing Gap and achieving your desired results.

The science

I'm reminded of the movie *'The Martian'* where Mark Watney, played by Matt Damon, says, *"In the face of overwhelming odds, I'm left with only one option: I'm gonna have to science the shit out of this."*

Companies grapple with the evolution of the workplace and the ever-changing needs of their talent. VUCA adds to the mounting challenges for leadership not armed with the right skills. My solution, the Human-first Performance Systems (HPS), delivers proven approaches with the perfected art of empowering leaders, teams, and entire organizations. One component of HPS is neuroscience-backed diagnostic tools developed by TTI Success Insights, the global leader in revealing human potential.

The science behind our talent diagnostic tools

As a licensed and certified partner of TTI Success Insights, our motto is: *We are different and proud of it.* Unlike our competition, the results are measurable, backed by over 35 years of research and validated by the neuroscience community. The Equal Employment Opportunity Commission (EEOC) and the Office of Contract Compliance Programs (OFCCP) have validated our tools to be 100% bias-free because of the rigorous data analysis by research teams and statisticians. More importantly, we back what we say. These and other qualifications led me to partner with TTISI.

Let's take a closer look at the five sciences available:

Science 1 of 5- Observable behaviors: Success in life, work, and relationships stems from understanding and having a sense of self, of deeply comprehending who you are, what you do, and how you do it. Behavior science helps you understand the HOW of your actions and decision-making.

Science 2 of 5- Motivators and Driving Forces: Motivators explain the WHY behind your actions and passions. This identifies the windows through which an individual views the world.

Science 3 of 5- Acumen: Possessing a high level of acumen means someone has the ability to make sound judgments and quick decisions due to their natural abilities and capacities.

Science 4 of 5- Competencies: While not every job requires the development of all 25 competencies, this science examines the level of each competency to identify which areas need to be developed further for a current or future role.

Science 5 of 5- Emotional intelligence (EQ): The ability to understand one's and other people's emotions in the decision-making process is critical in facilitating high levels of collaboration and productivity and achieving superior performance in the workplace and in personal relationships.

The tools and techniques

What gets measured gets done. Companies know that they can't do without measuring metrics to understand how the company is performing and if it is meeting its goals and objectives. Serious athletes measure their performance to determine how their training is going and whether they will meet the criteria for entering a competition. Think Olympics for boxing matches. What you don't measure doesn't matter. At least, that is what you convey when you don't truly know yourself. For example, one of several mistakes leaders make during a crisis is ineffective communication.

Write this down: We unknowingly fall into a trap called 'the illusion of communication.'

This concept is one that I've taught company leaders when communicating their mission both internally and externally. The scenario is one where leaders will share their mission and assume everyone will remember it. The fact is that it takes repetition and consistency over time. The best examples are a brand. A brand does not become a brand until consistency and ongoing repetition occur. This is why our brains will immediately recognize the Nike brand and slogan 'Just Do It.'

The most critical step is to start with your employees via internal communications. It has to be constant to the point where there is no doubt in your people's minds what you stand for. I've proven this to company leaders when I ask their employees about the company's mission. I've even proven it when I ask the company leader, who cannot state it because they wrote it a while back and forgot to live it in their daily decisions.

Coincidentally, it also directly correlates with underdeveloped listening skills. These, in addition to others, are directly measurable with my neuroscience-backed diagnostic tools.

Allow me to introduce my tools and share more stories.

- **Acumen Capacity Index – Utilizes 1 Science**

The Acumen Capacity Index (ACI) is based on the science of axiology. Axiology refers to the study of the nature of value and valuation. It explores how people interact with the world and how they see their value in the world. ACI measures how a person thinks and processes information. It measures a person's capacity and clarity of understanding of the world and themselves while revealing blind spots created by emotional biases. Understanding your thinking style and pinpointing emotional blind spots improves an individual's decision-making abilities significantly. The sophistication of ACI provides extraordinary benefits in four usage categories: Hiring and Selection Process, Defining Job Roles, Personal Development, and Management Coaching.

- **Job Benchmarking – Combines 4 Sciences**

Secure the talent necessary for success with this innovative talent management report. This patented solution is unique and effective because it benchmarks the specific job, not the person in the job. When appropriately implemented, it will directly affect your business's bottom line. You'll not only attract the best candidates but also save time and money by hiring the right people the first time and reducing the learning curve of the new employees strategically matched to fit your company. Of course, recruiters promise this benefit but have no quantifiable method for their recommendations. This solution empowers the entire team, not just the hiring manager, to more clearly quantify the job to identify selection criteria beyond the base skills needed for the position. Investing in Job Benchmarking will secure the talent necessary for success while eliminating common biases often associated with the hiring process. The Job Benchmark solution is architected to create the right combination of tools depending on whether the position is:

Entry level – When minimal skills are required for the job, but you want to know how they deal with problems and challenges, people and contacts, pace and consistency, and policies and constraints.

Managerial – When specific soft skills and experience are needed, the right talent, skill set, and competencies align with the job.

Executive and director level – When the position is critical to the organization and you need to know the talent's business acumen and decision-making process. It is important to understand higher-level attributes and characteristics such as: Is the individual aligned with the roles in their personal/professional life? How will the talent react to situations that directly or indirectly affect them? And can the individual make data-driven decisions but also score high in EQ and inspire colleagues and employees?

- **OD and 360 Performance – Combines 2 Sciences**

The need for an accurate and timely assessment of organizational development priorities has never been more important than in today's rapidly evolving workplace. Unlike the competition's labor-intensive survey offerings, ours saves time and effort **and can be done anywhere, anytime**. The patented Organizational Development and 360 Performance is an efficient alternative that allows your organization to identify the types of interventions required to grow quickly. We offer complete customizable features to measure what you need to know and are easily administered 24/7 through secure online access. Some popular applications are to increase employee engagement, receive 360 feedback, or gain valuable customer feedback.

- **Stress Quotient® – Combines 2 Sciences**

Do you feel like stress is harder to manage? You are not alone. Unmanaged stress gets in the way of your work and has serious health and cognitive impact. In 2019, 83% of U.S workers suffered work-related stress. Add in a pandemic, job or talent risks, and widespread economic uncertainty, and it makes sense why so many people feel overwhelmed. Stress-related ailments cost the nation $300 billion yearly in medical bills and lost productivity. There has never been a more critical time to accurately diagnose the seven types of stress across 17 sub-segments for an accurate snapshot of your organization's health. Individuals, teams, and entire organizations can use this tool to get an accurate snapshot of their stress levels in different categories, providing insights into the root cause. You can't fix anything unless you know the source of the problem in the first place. Leaders can create a combined team report result using their collective scores and finding the average. The assessment can also be used for an entire organization to get a company-wide score or can be used for individual teams and compared across departments. If one team is overly stressed while the rest of the organization isn't, it's time to re-evaluate roles and responsibilities.

- **EQ – Combines 3 Sciences**

There is never just one way to have EQ,
but there is always a reason to have it.

If you look at all the trends related to the Future of Work, a subject that I have presented on for years, you see that well-developed skills in emotional intelligence have made it to the top 10 most important skills required today as well as in the future. With rising levels of loneliness, depression, and mental health concerns, companies and leaders are looking for ways to re-engage their talent by fostering EQ assessments and training in their leadership. Companies are realizing that they have been shortsighted concerning the workforce. It stands to reason that workplace engagement is at an all-time low – even in pre-pandemic times. Business leaders failed to recognize the impact of their gaps. They believed that communicating their commitment to employee wellness was magically manifested, showing how out of rapport they were with their employees. This is why they cut funding for employee and leadership development and training. In brain science terms, this is another example of cognitive dissonance. The danger here is that the brain is a predictive brain, and cognitive dissonance stresses the brain because it cannot do its job, resulting in brain stress which can be directly linked to the surge of the workforce and economic trends like 'Quiet Quitting,' 'The Great Resignation,' and other buzzy management terms. The best leaders are making concerted efforts to regain trust and rapport with their employees. They are investing in becoming more emotionally intelligent, resilient, and adaptable leaders, but also investing in their teams to inspire and foster the next generation of leaders.

Story 1: Cognitive dissonance doesn't just happen in the workplace or amongst adults. When my son, Arthur, started kindergarten, we had just moved to San Diego. It was a good school, and the teacher was very nice, so it surprised me when Arthur started coming home halfway through the school year and going straight to bed. At first, we thought he was just tired from all the activities in school, but a month later, we received a letter from the teacher telling us she believed Arthur had a learning disability. She reported that he would not participate in the circle reading activities and not complete his assignments. We knew this was impossible because Arthur was gifted. At home, he had already shown command of multiplication of single digits. (Thank you, School House Rock educational videos!) In fact, I had seen one of the assignments the teacher showed us with his name, and none of the basic arithmetic problems were solved, including 1+2, 3+2, or 5+5. In the top right corner, my son wrote 9x9=81. It was clear Arthur was utterly bored and preferred to build something with LEGOs instead of participating in circle reading which was too basic for him.

The second element of this story is that we also discovered that a popular and charismatic student was bullying Arthur because he was too different from the other children. We learned about this from another parent who witnessed it. Arthur had never experienced this before, so his brain was stressed – cognitive dissonance. Further, the teacher had called attention to Arthur's non-cooperation in addition to the charismatic bully being her favorite. Additionally,

Arthur has extremely sensitive ears, later proven by his musical talent. He likely heard her share her opinions with room volunteers and others about him. For a child, this is a terrible experience and one that will stay with them if they don't have the support system they need. This teacher was not only biased but had a solid blind spot that prevented her from seeing Arthur's above-average talent and signaling that he was bored by writing 9x9=81. Instead of observing that he was talented but quiet, she saw a learning disability. I had to point this out to her in front of the school principal before she was willing to accept it.

In practical terms, whether it is employees or a gifted child such as Arthur, they go from believing to disbelieving, from respecting to disrespecting, from trusting to distrusting. And then leaders wonder why their teams are disengaged.

Story 2: Now let's consider the flip side of the impact a leader with a high EQ has on its employees. Companies struggled to get through the rough patch during the savings and loan financial crisis of the 80s and early 90s. I was at Hewlett Packard at the time, and the CEO, Lew Platt, announced a temporary pay cut across the board until economic conditions improved. Mr. Platt is a perfect example of a leader who incorporated EQ into his leadership strategy and communication. The result was a unified staff pulling together to elevate the company. I'm so proud to have experienced this level of EQ at the top and how it filtered down to every management level, as it inspired me to be that type of leader. His execution spoke volumes to all employees, which engendered trust and respect. It communicated:

- Situation: The state of the company during a time of crisis.

- Intent: Leadership was dedicated to pulling through and coming out stronger.

- Purpose: The need to call for a sacrifice from all of us during this tough time to avoid layoffs (a purpose with the employees in mind).

- Clarity: He asked staff employees to take a 5% pay cut, and all managers and executives would get a 10% pay cut. Hourly employees would see hours reduced in proportion to staff cuts.

- Unity: He asked us to stay united, and we would come out better and stronger on the other side. It was always a 'we' language pattern and 'asking for buyin', not demanding or expecting.

- Promise: He vowed to work harder than ever to reduce the pay cut period.

- Gratitude: He acknowledged the personal sacrifice and the impact on our families.

The inspiration and message of unity amongst employees created the sentiment that it wasn't just a 'yes' from us but a 'hell yes!' I'll take a pay cut to get us through this rough patch. The way it was strategized, communicated, and executed was brilliant. United, we were stronger, more productive, engaged, inspired, and more loyal than ever. And, as promised, salaries were restored after five months of collectively tightening our belts. In Chapter 7, I mentioned being proud of learning the value of DWYSYWD (Do What You Say You Will Do), and this exemplifies a leader not just talking the talk but walking the walk.

This type of leadership EQ has become rarer in the last three decades. The lack of investment in leadership and management training to improve their EQ scores is reflected in companies' decisions, which correlate with uninspired attitudes, low engagement levels, and lack of loyalty. Contrast that by imagining having your team or organization fully engaged, productive, and optimized. Imagine what you would accomplish. People with high Emotional Intelligence have been known to make better decisions and are recognized as better leaders. EQ is the most effective and essential skill for current and aspiring future leaders. Wouldn't investing in a solution that will yield you 7X-10X Return On Investment (ROI) be worth it? If so, reach out and I'll show you how.

Now consider reports from the National Institute of Mental Health in January 2020 showed that emerging generations 18-25 years old have the highest prevalence of serious mental illness compared to other age groups.[56] Based on research and trends I've observed, I can see why Gen Z is described as the loneliest generation, with 73% reporting that they sometimes or constantly feel alone.[57]

One distinction about Gen Z-ers compared to previous generations is that they are the first true digital natives with no experience or knowledge of life without digital devices. Today's leaders and the future of leadership in general face unique challenges not found in existing leadership playbooks. These playbooks need to be upgraded to meet current and future challenges in a creative and inspiring way.

To achieve leadership excellence and a high EQ, we need to clear up some misconceptions. For example, some people equate EQ with empathy. However, empathy is only one of several EQ's skill components. Other misconceptions about empathy include that empathy means always being nice, is a sign of weakness, or that you have to get in the uncomfortable emotional gutter with the other person. Every one of these is so far from that truth that it is almost sad to see.

---

56 https://www.nimh.nih.gov/health/statistics/mental-illness
57 https://www.psychologytoday.com/us/blog/the-case-con-nection/202208/3-things-making-gen-z-the-loneliest-genera-tion#:~:text=Seventy-three%20percent%20of%20Gen,think%20they%20prefer%20instant%20message.

EMPATHY

WHAT IT IS NOT

WHAT IT IS

- Seeing the person as a human being, just like me
- Actively listening without judgment
- Sensing and understanding other people's emotions
- Holding space for others to share their feelings
- Seeing things from the person's perspective
- Validating other's feelings
- Showing concern for others

- Being courteous, having manners, or having a calming voice
- One-upping with your experience
- Assuming I know how the person feels based on my own experiences
- Telling the person things will get better
- Feeling sorry for the person, that's sympathy
- It is not a sign of weakness

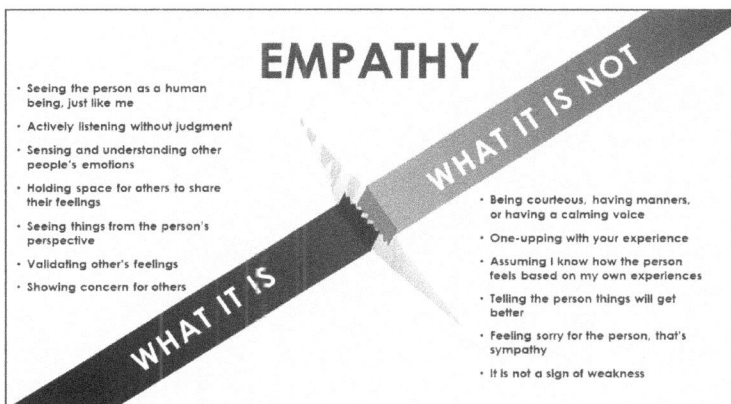

Distinguishing what empathy is and what it is not

Empathy does not mean being courteous, having good manners, or a nice calming voice. It is not generosity nor a sign of weakness. In fact, empathy requires the courage to take someone else's perspective and peek into what they are going through without joining them in their own pit of despair. Now more than ever, it is critical for clients to understand their Emotional Quotient. It is an assessment tool that **helps you build the skills to sense, understand, and effectively apply the power of emotions** to facilitate higher levels of collaboration and productivity. With EQ training, you and your employees will develop the skills and knowledge to better understand customers or internal stakeholders, manage their expectations, and ultimately meet their needs. An impact/case study, one of my clients stated, "*After assessing our staff, implementing EQ training, and working on employees' specific work strategies, we saw a 25% increase in annual profits.*"

Emotional Discipline

Nothing happens without discipline (from my article: *'EQ is Important – Now Go Measure It! 5 Things I learned From Measuring Mine.'*)[58]

In practical terms, discipline has been the practice of training people to obey rules or a code of conduct. It may also mean a punishment. Discipline is used to gain what's coveted. The concept is still honored and honorable. For instance, it applies when developing a perfectly sculpted body. And for those who want this, they will go to great lengths to get it. The same applies to those training for a marathon, the Olympics, or other monumental achievements that require very high discipline, whether in sports, business, or life.

Emotional discipline, however, is an entirely different beast. It is about **resisting the impulse** to send that flaming email you'd regret later or running the other way when tough decisions must be made. Lacking emotional discipline has consequences such as **emotional hijacking**. We've all been there at some point, right? After all, we are emotional human beings, not robots. Not yet, anyway.

The point is to minimize instances that can derail your success. Peter Bregman nails this concept of emotional

---

58 https://www.linkedin.com/pulse/emotional-intelligence-import-ant-now-go-measure-adriana-vela/

discipline in his book *"Leading With Emotional Courage: How to Have Hard Conversations, Create Accountability, and Inspire Actions On Your Most Important Work."* Emotional discipline, also known as intrinsic motivation, could be the key to unlocking the outcomes we want and is a measurable dimension of the best EQ assessments. Intrinsic motivation is a critical indicator of how long it might take to see results.

What about emotional granularity, and why is this important? Emotions are extremely powerful and dominate your view of a situation, a person, or your world. Emotional granularity isn't just about having a rich vocabulary; it's about experiencing the world, and yourself, more precisely. It can make a difference in your life. In fact, there is growing scientific evidence that precisely tailored emotional experiences are good for you, even if those experiences are negative.[59] According to a collection of studies, finely-grained, unpleasant feelings allow people to become more agile at regulating their emotions,[60] less likely to drink excessively[61] when stressed, and less likely to retaliate aggressively[62] against someone who has hurt them.

---

59 https://www.affective-science.org/pubs/2015/kash-dan-et-all-unpacking-emotion-differentiation-2015.pdf

60 https://www.affective-science.org/pubs/2001/01MaprelationDif-fReg.pdf

61 https://journals.sagepub.com/doi/abs/10.1177/0956797610379863

62 https://pubmed.ncbi.nlm.nih.gov/22023359/

Engagement Insights Report

"Employee disengagement translates to a profit loss of 34% of the disengaged employees' annual salary." - Forbes

If you want to retain your best talent and increase employee engagement, this report is an intuitive, accessible, practical, and succinct tool to start with. It serves as a guidebook for managing the reboarding process and is the best tool for engaging, reboarding, reconnecting, and optimizing your organization.

Employee disengagement has been a growing problem for companies. The workplace disconnect needs a new solution. The solutions that Human Resource departments or consultants provide are hit-and-miss. Why? Because they have not taken the steps or have the proper tools to measure the areas and root causes of disengagement accurately. This is like throwing darts blindfolded or shaking a tree to see what falls. Worse yet, in desperation to 'fix' the problem, they resort to the unproven promise of AI tools. Engagement, or lack thereof, is a human issue, but do we want an AI to teach us how to be more human? Should we ask AI to raise our children as well? The scary reality is that robotics is yesterday's video entertainment.

What is needed is a human-first solution, not artificial sugar. Employers need to be honest with themselves and realize that their employees work because they need to, not because there's no place they'd rather be. Employers also need to know that they have a great deal of control over whether or not their workforce remains engaged. Even at the "all-time high" employment rate, 53% of US workers remained disengaged. Fast-forward to our COVID-induced VUCA world, and the trends point to a mass exodus of the workforce leaving their jobs in search of others that align with their values and needs. Organizations that want to retain their talent will focus on helping employees develop a path toward their professional and personal goals. The need for employee engagement and excellent communication is higher than ever.

Talent Insights – Two Sciences for Individuals, Management, Sales Teams, and Executives

"By implementing Talent Insights in our company's hiring process, we slashed our turnover rate in half, saving the company >$500,000 a year."

The Talent Insights® report is ideal for recruiting, retaining, and developing employees customized for all levels, including executives, management/staff, and sales teams. It is simple yet sophisticated. It measures behaviors and driving forces and then effortlessly integrates those two sciences to identify the HOW and the WHY people do what they do. This allows leaders, managers, and organizations to determine their fit in the organization, how they add diversity and balance the team, and how best to further support, develop, and engage them. Learn HOW you do what you do and WHY you do what you do by measuring behaviors and driving forces/motivators.

There is no other talent assessment out there that matches Talent Insights in terms of validity, accuracy, compliance, and continued research and improvement and that has neuroscience validation. I'm obsessed with providing the best solutions to my clients, so I picked TTI as a partner based on the characteristics below.

Bringing it all together

As I close this last chapter, I reflect on the journey I've laid out for you and am grateful you have joined me. My mission to improve the human condition by transforming leadership overwhelm into agility and adaptability for growth in an increasingly complex world is unwavering. Together, we have toured areas of our brain to set the stage and remind you that our brains are amazing three-pound organs at the seat of intelligence, interpreters of the senses, initiators of body movement, and controllers of behavior. The brain reflects our humanity. The brain's non-physical counterpart is our soul, which leads us to ultimate happiness and peace. This book aims to empower you by presenting the magic of seeing the relationship between the two: brain and soul. More importantly, I wanted to show you that our actions have a silent but direct impact on our soul, and taking care of it can awaken tremendous power in you. All you need to do is connect to it.

With those two critical anchors, we have journeyed through areas like the neuroscience of fear and the best ways to conquer it, the limitations of the Growth Mindset to empower you with distinctions, and how social pain is real pain so that you can understand yourself and others much better. Similarly, the concept of toxic positivity helps you identify and address this behavior more effectively or change your behavior if you are an unintentional culprit. Next on the tour was visiting the land of the dark side of innovation with the goal of providing plenty of food for thought, given our technology-driven society. Before this last chapter, the last stop was the challenge to reframe your relationship with failure.

As humans, we are designed for growth, and growth depends on learning and understanding as many perspectives as possible. Without it, we will wither in the sea of sameness.

If you are curious about how you can achieve your greatest goals and live the life you want, I've prepared a set of bonuses and invite you to download them at https://BrainSciencefortheSoul.com